GENERAL EQUILIBRIUM

By the same author
EQUILIBRIUM AND DISEQUILIBRIUM

GENERAL EQUILIBRIUM

MICHAEL ALLINGHAM
London School of Economics

A HALSTED PRESS BOOK

JOHN WILEY & SONS
New York–Toronto

© Michael Allingham 1975

All rights reserved. No part of this publication may be reproduced or transmitted, in any form or by any means, without permission

First published in the United Kingdom 1975 by
THE MACMILLAN PRESS LTD
London and Basingstoke

Published in the U.S.A. and Canada
by Halsted Press, a Division
of John Wiley & Sons, Inc.
New York

Printed in Great Britain

Library of Congress Cataloging in Publication Data

Allingham, Michael.
   General equilibrium.

   "A Halsted Press book."
   Includes index.
   1. Equilibrium (Economics)   I. Title.
HB145.A45   1975   330'.01'8   75–17842
ISBN 0–470–02493–3

To Jane and Daniel

Contents

Preface	ix
1 SCOPE AND METHOD	
1.1 Basic Ideas	1
1.2 Historical Overview	2
1.3 Mathematical Preliminaries	4
1.4 Euclidean Space	5
1.5 Linear Maps	8
Notes	11
Problems	12
2 INDIVIDUAL AGENTS	
2.1 Commodities	13
2.2 Preferences	14
2.3 Demand	17
2.4 Production Sets	21
2.5 Supply	24
Notes	25
Problems	26
3 COMPETITIVE EQUILIBRIUM	
3.1 Concepts	27
3.2 Existence	30
3.3 Optimality	32
3.4 Uniqueness	36
3.5 Production	38
Notes	41
Problems	42
4 CO-OPERATIVE EQUILIBRIUM	
4.1 Edgeworth Box	44
4.2 The Core	46
4.3 Asymptotic Core	48
4.4 Edgeworth's Conjecture	51

viii CONTENTS

4.5	Production	52
Notes		54
Problems		54

5 DYNAMIC EQUILIBRIUM

5.1	Concepts	56
5.2	Abstract Framework	57
5.3	Monopoly	60
5.4	Existence	63
5.5	Properties	66
Notes		69
Problems		69

6 STABILITY

6.1	Tatonnement	70
6.2	Lyapounov Method	72
6.3	Global Stability	74
6.4	Local Stability	78
6.5	Dynamic Equilibrium	79
Notes		81
Problems		81

7 COMPARATIVE STATICS

7.1	Parameter Changes	83
7.2	Substitutability	85
7.3	Hicksian Cross	89
7.4	Correspondence Principle	91
7.5	Dynamic Equilibrium	95
Notes		95
Problems		96

APPENDIX: SOCIAL PREFERENCE

A.1 Social Choice	99
A.2 Decisiveness	101
A.3 Pareto Function	103
Notes	104
Notation	107
Index	111

Preface

The aim of this book is to provide a systematic exposition of general equilibrium theory in a simple yet rigorous framework. To this end, the presentation follows three principles. Firstly, the framework is based on interpretable axioms: thus simplifications which have no clear economic justification are avoided. Secondly, all propositions are proved, but in the simplest meaningful versions: thus more technical generalisations are omitted from the main discussion, though mentioned in the notes. Finally, the argument is concise, though quite informal: thus various minor points are left to the problems.

The book is addressed primarily to advanced undergraduate or beginning graduate students following such courses as 'general equilibrium', 'further microeconomics' or 'mathematical economics'. The treatment is essentially self-contained, and assumes no prior knowledge of economics, or, beyond the most basic ideas, of mathematics.

Some of the material covered in the book has formed the basis of lectures at the University of Essex, Northwestern University, the University of Pennsylvania and the London School of Economics. I am grateful to many colleagues at these and other institutions for their comments, particularly to Kotaro Suzumura for reading the complete text in proof.

London M A
March 1975

General Equilibrium

1 Scope and Method

This book seeks to explain the essence of economic science through general equilibrium theory. It considers questions which appear highly abstract, yet which are of real relevance. What is the best form of economic organisation? What are the economic effects of non-economic phenomena? Such are the basic questions of normative and positive economic enquiry. Before coming to terms with them we consider the scope of our enquiry, and the method of attack.

1.1 BASIC IDEAS

Perhaps the most satisfactory definition of economics is that it is what economists are interested in. We shall not attempt to improve on this circular definition, but merely outline what they may find of interest in this book.

We are concerned with society, as a collection of individuals, each of whom has wants and constraints. Each individual acts in accordance with his wants and constraints, either independently or in co-operation with others; but of course this changes the constraints affecting other individuals. Thus individuals in society necessarily interact: this interaction, occasioned by the basic conflict between wants and constraints, is the subject of this book. This is particularly applied to the material sphere, that is to individuals' interaction in the exchange and production of commodities.

Apart from its intrinsic interest the study of economics is relevant from both the normative and positive viewpoints. Normative results concern the efficiency, desirability, and fairness of the economic system; they form the basis for such ideological debates as that of capitalism versus socialism. Positive results concern the economic effects of government or external action; they form the basis for such practical debates as that of taxation versus government expenditure. (Of course these two viewpoints are not distinct: most interesting economic questions have both normative and positive aspects.)

The study of economics may be approached from the micro or

macro perspectives, as well as from general equilibrium. Microeconomics examines the economic behaviour of isolated individuals, taking their wants and constraints as given; it therefore avoids the basic question of the interaction between individuals, though it is a useful starting point for this. Macroeconomics, on the other hand, studies the economic behaviour of society as a whole, examining the aggregates of individual behaviour; thus it too avoids the study of the interaction between individuals, yet suggests a goal, or ending point, for this.

Since we consider society as a collection of individuals the rigorous study of society must be based on axioms relating to individuals. At the same time the fruits of such a study should be capable of relating to society as a whole. Microeconomics starts and ends with individuals, while macroeconomics starts and ends with society: general equilibrium analysis, however, bridges the two, starting with individuals and ending with society.

1.2 HISTORICAL OVERVIEW

The subject matter of the various chapters of this book (excluding this and the following chapter, which lay some foundations) may usefully be surveyed from an historical perspective.

Although an indefinite string of precursors exists, the founding of economics in its full general equilibrium sense is unmistakably attributable to Walras in the 1870s. The lasting value of Walras' contribution lies in the framework he specified and the questions he posed. The basic framework consists of a number of commodities with associated prices, and a number of consumers and producers. Producers purchase commodities and transform these into other commodities which they sell; they do this so as to maximise their profits, at some given prices, subject to their given production possibilities. Consumers exchange commodities with each other and with producers to obtain a most desirable, in some given sense, consumption bundle, subject to the value, at the given prices, of their purchases not exceeding that of their sales plus their shares in the producers' profits.

Walras' first problem (discussed in Chapter 3) concerned the existence of a *competitive equilibrium*, that is a set of prices at which all this independent optimising behaviour would be in some sense consistent. Walras attempted to answer this by investigating the numbers of equations and of variables in the system, but did not succeed. A rigorous examination of the problem did not take place until the 1930s, when a number of writers recognised that the problem was deeper than one of counting equations and variables. The problem was solved then, but in a relatively narrow form and in a somewhat complex way. It was not until the development of certain fixed-point theorems in mathematics that this result was able to be generalised and simplified. This occurred in the 1950s, in the classical works of Debreu and others. From the time of Adam Smith it has been conjectured that a self-determining decentralised economy is an 'efficient' form of economic organisation, or that a competitive equilibrium is an 'optimal' state. This important property of the competitive equilibrium was demonstrated at the same time as existence by Debreu and others in the 1950s. The additional question of the uniqueness of this equilibrium was solved in the original existence work of the 1930s.

A completely different approach to general equilibrium (discussed in Chapter 4) originates with the ideas of Edgeworth in the 1880s, but was not formalised until the development of game theory in mathematics in the 1940s and 1950s. In this approach consumers and producers may co-operate with each other in any way they choose, and all exchanges are through bargaining, rather than trade at given prices. The central concept is that of a *co-operative equilibrium*, that is a state which cannot be bettered, for themselves, by any group of individuals. The existence of such a state and the basic property that this is approximately the same as the competitive equilibrium was shown in the 1950s and 1960s, notably by Aumann.

Yet a third approach to general equilibrium (discussed in Chapter 5) investigates the concept of a *dynamic equilibrium*, that is a state from which there is no movement, rather than one which is consistent. Clearly this requires the specification of the laws of movement, and is therefore essentially monopolistic, unlike the competitive equilibrium which is competitive in the sense that no individual can move prices. This idea is implicit in the work of Debreu in the early 1950s; it is developed explicitly in this book.

Walras' second problem (discussed in Chapter 6) concerned the *stability* of equilibrium, that is whether the economy would ever attain its equilibrium, or equivalently, would return to equilibrium if temporarily disturbed from it. Since the competitive equilibrium is static this clearly requires the introduction of some dynamic process: Walras specified a 'tatonnement', in which prices were adjusted according to the state of the provisional market. Walras was not able to solve this problem completely, and it was returned to in the 1940s by Hicks and Samuelson, but only for 'small' disturbances from equilibrium. The problem was solved for 'large' disturbances by Morishima and others in the 1950s and 1960s.

Walras' final problem (discussed in Chapter 7) concerned the *comparative statics* of equilibrium, that is how the equilibrium state would be affected by changes in the underlying attributes of the economy: preferences, resources, share ownership, and production possibilities. Little specific progress was made on this by Walras, and the problem was returned to in the 1940s by Hicks and Samuelson in connection with their stability work. Again this was only for small changes; the effects of large changes were examined in the 1960s by Morishima and others.

The normative property of optimality or *social preference* (discussed in the Appendix) is interpreted in general equilibrium theory in the sense proposed by Pareto in the 1890s. This has always been the predominant interpretation in economics, though the value judgements underlying it have only been thoroughly explored recently in the work of Arrow, Sen, and others in the 1960s and 1970s.

1.3 MATHEMATICAL PRELIMINARIES

To obtain a proper understanding of economic society we must proceed in a logical manner. The particular aspects of logic which transpire to be the most appropriate are predominantly mathematical, so much of the discussion is framed in mathematical language, but simply as a mode of logical expression: the study is of economics, not mathematics.

It is helpful to review the mathematical ideas to be drawn on, but from a strictly applied viewpoint. Thus only the minimum mathematical background for the economic analysis is presented, and all extensions and generalisations are ignored, which means that a simpler terminology than the standard may sometimes be employed; however, all the necessary mathematics is included. For the same reason the emphasis is on definition and explanation, and formal proofs are omitted.

It is neither useful nor practical to start with the ultimate foundations of logic and mathematics. Instead, the basic notions are taken as familiar. It is, however, helpful to make clear exactly what is to be assumed: this section outlines this material without explanation (other than to avoid possible ambiguity of terminology). In short, this understanding is simply that of the concepts and mechanical manipulation of sets, numbers, vectors, functions, and matrices.

The primary concept is that of a set, as a collection of elements. Sets may be compared by equality or by one being a subset of the other, and may be combined by taking unions, intersections, complements or differences, and products. There may be an ordering of the elements of a set, or a partial ordering (an 'ordering' which does not require all elements to be comparable).

Particular sets are the sets of positive integers, of complex numbers

(numbers with real and imaginary parts), and the set R of real numbers. Real numbers may be combined by addition or multiplication (or their inverse operations, subtraction and division). They may be partially ordered by the relations '$=$' and '$\geqq$'; $\alpha > \beta$ if $\alpha \geqq \beta$ but $\alpha \neq \beta$, while $\alpha < \beta$ if $\beta > \alpha$, and so forth. A non-empty subset of R may have a maximum and a minimum in the sense of the ordering '$\geqq$'.

If n is a positive integer the product of R with itself $n-1$ times is the n-dimensional Euclidean space R^n, an element x of which is a vector $(x_1, \ldots x_n)$. Vectors may be added or multiplied by a number (to produce another vector) or two may be combined with each other to produce a number (their inner product). They may be partially ordered by the relations '$=$' and '$\geqq$' (defined componentwise); '$>$' is also defined componentwise and $x \geq y$ if $x \geqq y$ but $x \neq y$.

A function is a rule identifying with each element of its domain some unique element of its range; if the process can be reversed the function has an inverse. Functions may be added, multiplied by a number, or composed. A particular function is a linear function: if this maps from R^n to itself it may be represented by an $n \times n$ matrix which operates on, or multiplies, one vector to obtain another. Matrices are combined as are functions. An $n \times n$ matrix has cofactors and a determinant, which may define its inverse (the inverse function).

We use these basic notions to present the further mathematical ideas to be used, firstly as applied to Euclidean space in general, and then to linear maps defined on this.

1.4 EUCLIDEAN SPACE

The set of extended numbers comprises the elements of R together with the symbol ∞ (infinity). If $\alpha \in R$ we understand that $\alpha + \infty = \infty$, $\alpha - \infty = -\infty$ (a definition), $\alpha\infty = \infty$ if $\alpha > 0$, $\alpha\infty = -\infty$ if $\alpha < 0$, and so forth, with $-\infty < \alpha < \infty$. Henceforth, we fix a positive integer n and denote the product of the set of extended numbers with itself $n-1$ times by E, the extended Euclidean space. Relevant subsets of E are the non-negative orthant

$$\Omega = \{x \in E | x \geqq 0\}$$

and the positive orthant

$$\Omega_+ = \{x \in E | x > 0\}.$$

Since we shall be exclusively concerned with subsets of E (or of the set of extended numbers), we denote such sets as Ω simply as

$$\{x | x \geqq 0\},$$

and so forth. The norm of a point x is the square root of its inner product with itself, that is

$$\|x\| = (xx)^{1/2},$$

and the distance between two points x and y is the norm of their difference, that is

$$\rho(x, y) = \|x - y\|.$$

A sequence is an endless succession of elements, or formally a function from the positive integers to E, denoted x^1, x^2, ..., or simply x^t, where $t = 1, 2, \ldots$. The sequence x^t has a limit $\bar{x}$ if sufficiently extreme elements of the sequence remain arbitrarily close to $\bar{x}$, that is $x^t \to \bar{x}$ if for every $\delta > 0$ there is some $T < \infty$ such that

$$\rho(x^t, \bar{x}) < \delta$$

whenever $t > T$; this is ensured if

$$\rho(x^s, x^t) < \delta$$

whenever $s, t > T$. For example, in R the sequence

$$a^t = 2^{-t}$$

tends to the limit zero, but the sequence

$$a^t = 2^t$$

has no limit.

A set S is closed if no sequence contained in the set has a limit outside the set, that is if $x^t \in S$ for every t and $x^t \to \bar{x}$ imply $\bar{x} \in S$; thus Ω is closed but Ω_+ is not. A set S is bounded if all its elements are a finite distance from the origin, 0, that is if there is some $k < \infty$ such that

$$\rho(x, 0) < k$$

for every $x \in S$: thus the cube

$$\{x \mid 0 < x_i < 1 \text{ for each } i\}$$

is bounded but Ω is not. A set S is weakly convex if the line joining any two of its elements is in the set, that is if

$$z = ax + (1 - a)y \in S$$

whenever $x, y \in S$ ($x \neq y$) and $0 < a < 1$; it is convex if such a line is in the 'interior' of the set, that is if, for some $\delta > 0$,

$$\{z' \mid \rho(z, z') < \delta\} \subset S.$$

Weakly convex (S), convex (T), and non-convex ($S \cup T$) sets are illustrated in Figure 1.1, which also shows that the union of convex sets need not be convex. However, apart from this the taking of the union, intersection or product of two sets retains closedness, boundedness and convexity, while taking the sum retains boundedness and convexity.

A function f is continuous if it preserves limits in the sense that for

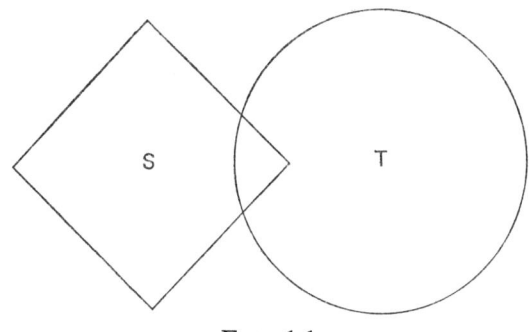

FIG. 1.1

any sequence with a limit the limit of the images is the image of the limit, that is if $x^t \to \bar{x}$ implies

$$f(x^t) \to f(\bar{x})$$

(written more simply as

$$f(x) \to f(\bar{x})$$

as $x \to \bar{x}$). For example, the function g from R to R defined by

$$g(a) = -a^2$$

is continuous but that defined by

$$h(a) = 1/a \text{ if } a \neq 0,$$
$$h(0) = 0$$

is not. A real-valued function f (on a convex set) is quasi-convex if for every a the set

$$\{x \mid f(x) \leq a\}$$

is convex; f is quasi-concave if the equivalent set with the inequality reversed is convex. Thus the function g above is quasi-convex, but h is neither quasi-convex nor quasi-concave. These are illustrated in Figure 1.2. Taking the sum or composition of functions retains continuity but not quasi-convexity.

We use these concepts in three important theorems: Weierstrass' theorem states that a continuous real-valued function on a non-empty closed bounded set has a maximum and a minimum. Minkowski's

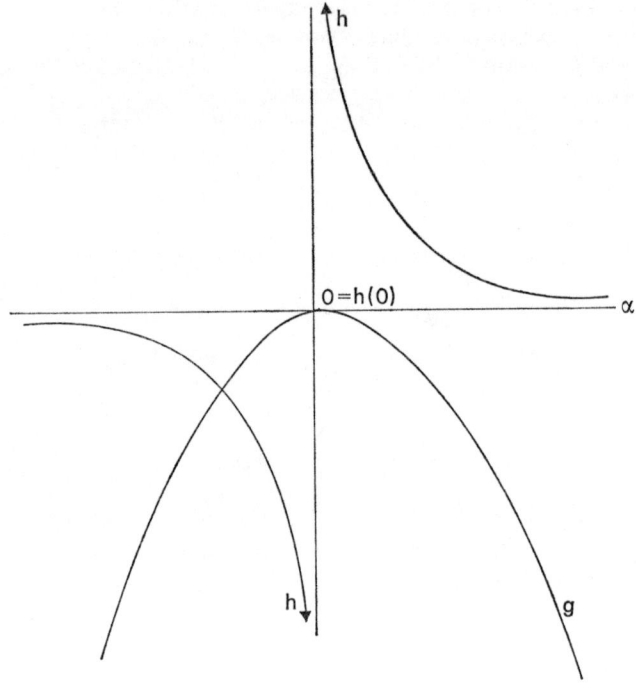

Fig. 1.2

theorem states that if S is a convex set containing no negative point then there is some vector $p \geq 0$ such that $px \geqq 0$ for every $x \in S$; here p is the normal of the hyperplane

$$H = \{x \mid px = 0\}$$

separating S from the negative orthant. Brouwer's theorem states that if f is a continuous function from the set

$$Q_m = \{x \in \Omega \mid xe = m\}$$

to itself (for any $m > 0$) then there is some $\bar{x}$ such that $\bar{x} = f(\bar{x})$; here Q_m is the simplex of those non-negative vectors summing to m (e is the unit vector $(1, \ldots 1)$), and $\bar{x}$ is a fixed point of f. These three theorems are illustrated in Figures 1.3. to 1.5.

1.5 LINEAR MAPS

A function F is linear if

$$F(x + y) = F(x) + F(y)$$

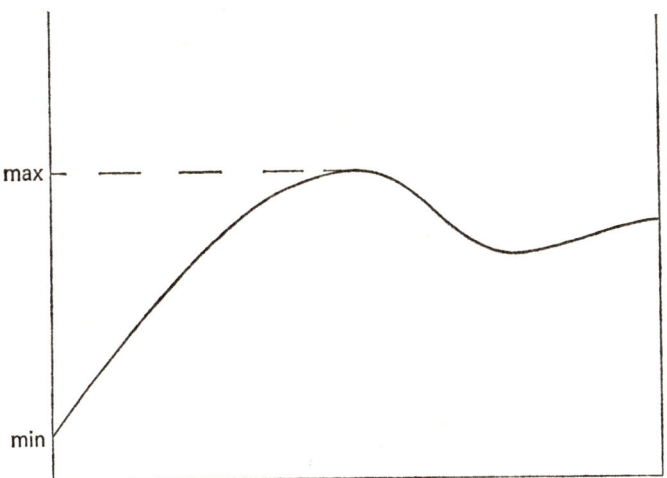

Fig. 1.3

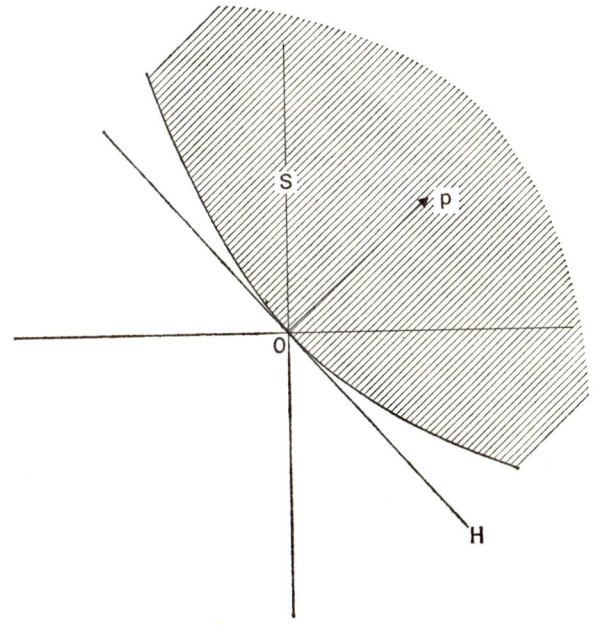

Fig. 1.4

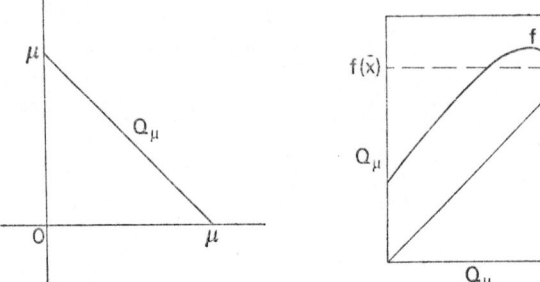

FIG. 1.5

for all x and y, and

$$F(ax) = aF(x)$$

when $a \in R$. A linear function or map from R^n to R^m is identified with an $m \times n$ matrix, so we consider F as a matrix and write $F(x)$ as Fx. For example, the only linear maps from R to R are those of the form

$$F(a) = \lambda a$$

where $\lambda \in R$: F is equivalent to the 1×1 matrix $[\lambda]$, or λ.

We may frequently approximate an arbitrary continuous function f at some point $\bar{x}$ by a linear map F, in the sense that, for any h, the difference between

$$f(\bar{x} + h) - f(\bar{x})$$

and

$$F(\bar{x} + h) - F(\bar{x}) = Fh$$

is small relative to h: specifically,

$$f(\bar{x} + h) - f(\bar{x}) - Fh = \delta(h)$$

where

$$\|\delta(h)\|/\|h\| \to 0$$

as $h \to 0$. If this is possible the function f is differentiable (at $\bar{x}$) and the linear map, or matrix, F is its derivative, or Jacobian. For example, we may approximate the function f from R to R defined by

$$f(a) = a^2$$

at the point $a = 1$ by the matrix $[2]$, in that

$$(1 + h)^2 - 1 - 2h = h^2$$

and

$$\|h^2\|/\|h\| = |h| \to 0$$

as $h \to 0$.

If f is a differentiable function from R^n to R which has a maximum (or minimum) at some point $\bar{x}$ then the Jacobian of f at $\bar{x}$, which is an $1 \times n$ matrix, must be zero, for otherwise an increase (or decrease) could be attained in some direction. For example, the function f from R to R defined by
$$f(a) = -a^2$$
has a maximum at the point $a = 0$, where its Jacobian is the matrix [0].

Henceforth, we consider linear maps from E to E, or square matrices. Relevant square matrices $A = [a_{ij}]$ are positive matrices (where each $a_{ij} > 0$), positive diagonal matrices (where each $a_{ii} > 0$ and $a_{ij} = 0$ when $i \neq j$), symmetric matrices (where each $a_{ij} = a_{ji}$), and positive definite matrices (symmetric matrices where $x(Ax) > 0$ for all $x \neq 0$). For example, the identity matrix I is not positive but is positive diagonal, symmetric, and positive definite. Negative properties are defined similarly.

A complex number λ is a characteristic root of a square matrix A if
$$Ax = \lambda x$$
for some non-zero x, or equivalently if the determinant $|A - \lambda I|$ is zero. If all the characteristic roots of A have negative real parts then the matrix
$$e^{tA} = I + tA + \tfrac{1}{2}t^2 A^2 + \ldots$$
tends to the null matrix as $t \to \infty$, so that A is a stable matrix. For example, the matrix $-I$ has the unique characteristic root -1, so is stable:
$$e^{-tI} = I(1 - t + \tfrac{1}{2}t^2 - \ldots) \to 0$$

We use these concepts in two important theorems. The Routh-Hurwitz theorem states that if A is a stable $n \times n$ matrix then the trace (the sum of the diagonal elements) of A^{-1} is negative and the determinant $|A|$ has sign $(-1)^{n-1}$. The Frobenius theorem states that a positive matrix A has a real maximal characteristic root λ^*, and that $(A - aI)^{-1}$ is a negative matrix whenever $a > \lambda^*$.

Notes

1 References to the historical works mentioned here are given in context in later chapters. Comparable books on general equilibrium are, in approximate increasing order of complexity: E. R. Weintraub [*General Equilibrium Theory*, London, 1974], J. Quirk and R. Saposnik [*Introduction to General Equilibrium Theory and Welfare Economics*, New York, 1968], G. Debreu [*Theory of Value*, New York, 1959], K. J. Arrow and F. H. Hahn [*General*

Competitive Analysis, San Francisco, 1971] T. Rader, [*Theory of General Economic Equilibrium*, New York, 1972] and W. Hildenbrand [*Core and Equilibria of a Large Economy*, Princeton, 1974]. Of these Weintraub is perhaps the best preparation for this book, with Arrow and Hahn the best successor.

2 The mathematics presented here is quite standard; further explanation, generalisations, and proofs may be found in most analysis or algebra texts, or equivalently in a modern 'mathematics for economics' text, for example E. Klein [*Mathematical Methods in Theoretical Economics*, New York, 1973].

Problems

1 Show that if a sequence has a limit then this is unique.
2 Show that any $\alpha \in R$ may be approximated by the ratio of two integers, that is for any $\delta > 0$ there are two integers m and n such that
$$|\alpha - m/n| < \delta.$$
3 Show that taking the union, intersection or product of two sets retains closedness and boundedness.
4 Show that taking the intersection, product, or sum of two sets retains convexity and weak convexity.
5 Show that taking the sum or composition of two functions retains continuity.
6 Show that if a function has a derivative at some point then this is unique.
7 If λ is a characteristic root of a matrix A show that it is a characteristic root of any similar matrix, that is a matrix CAC^{-1} for any non-singular matrix C.
8 Show that a stable matrix is non-singular.
9 Show that a negative definite matrix is stable.
10 Construct examples to show that the sum of closed sets need not be closed nor the sum of quasi-convex functions quasi-convex.

2 Individual Agents

Economics was interpreted in Chapter 1 as the study of society as a collection of individuals who pursue their own ends, either independently or in co-operation with others, yet who necessarily interact in so doing; this is applied particularly to their interaction in the material sphere, or their exchange and production of commodities. We now consider more precisely the nature of the actions of the individual agents, and of the commodities to which these refer.

2.1 COMMODITIES

The essence of a commodity is taken to be understood: loosely, as some physical or intangible entity which is considered to be directly or indirectly desirable, and which is alienable. One commodity is distinguished from another if, for any reason, any individual considers them to be different. The main reasons for distinction will then be physical nature, quality (whether intrinsic or 'status-giving', real or imagined), location, and date. Thus, for example, wheat would not only be distinguished from labour, but also according to whether it were hard or soft, delivered in London or New York, available today or tomorrow, or any combination of these. Such distinction will be sufficient for the immediate analysis, though in Chapter 5 we shall also distinguish commodities by ownership (note that alienability requires ownership).

We assume there to be a finite number, n, of commodities, indexed by $i = 1, \ldots n$. Each commodity is measured in some given physical units, and is assumed to be infinitely divisible. If we have a bundle of commodities consisting of q_1 units of commodity 1, q_2 of 2, and so on, we may represent this by the n-tuple $q = (q_1, \ldots q_n)$. Clearly q is an element of (n-dimensional) Euclidean space E, and because of divisibility any point in E is associated with some commodity bundle. Thus the set of commodity bundles, or the commodity space, is E.

Since commodities are desired they will typically be transferred between individuals only in exchange for other commodities. If q_i

units of commodity i are exchanged for q_j of j then the price of commodity i in terms of j is q_j/q_i (or the price of j in terms of i is q_i/q_j). Thus prices are relative. However, for ease of interpretation we may consider commodities to be exchanged, or bought and sold, in terms of some abstract unit of account: then, if one unit of commodity is exchangeable for p_i units of account the (accounting) price of commodity i is p_i. The prices of the various commodities may then be represented by the price system or price, $p = (p_1, \ldots p_n)$. Clearly p is an element of E; since all commodities are desirable we need not consider negative prices, so that in fact p is an element of Ω, the non-negative orthant of E. Again, any point in Ω is associated with a price, so the price space is Ω.

2.2 PREFERENCES

The essence of an individual agent in the economy is taken to be understood: loosely, as a human or abstract choice-making entity. Agents are distinguished by their existence, and are partitioned into two classes. Those in the former, which we may think of as households or consumers, make choices concerning their consumption of commodities, while those in the latter, which we may think of as firms or producers, make choices concerning their production of commodities. The role of an agent is to make a choice, or take an action: specifically, he takes the most preferred action of those available.

We first consider consumers, and specify what is meant by action, preference, and availability for a consumer. As indicated, a consumer's action is the choice of the amounts of the various commodities he is to consume. This choice, denoted $x = (x_1, \ldots x_n)$, is his consumption, which is of course an element of E; in fact, by its nature consumption is non-negative, so that the consumption space is Ω. This concept of consumption is wide, and, for example, embraces 'saving', or the consumption of future-dated commodities.

The concept of preference relevant to consumption is that of some relation over all possible consumptions, which we denote by $\bar{\pi}$. If x and x' are two consumptions and $x\bar{\pi}x'$ then x is considered weakly preferred to x'; if $x\bar{\pi}x'$ and $x'\bar{\pi}x$ then x is considered indifferent to x', written $x \sim x'$; finally, if $x\bar{\pi}x'$ but we do not have $x \sim x'$, then x is considered preferred to x', written $x\pi x'$.

Not all relations could reasonably be interpreted as preference relations. Firstly, we should not allow a consumption to be preferred to itself. Secondly, we should require all consumptions to be comparable in some way. Thirdly, we should require that if one consumption is weakly preferred to another which in turn is weakly preferred to a third, then the original consumption should be weakly preferred to the third. Thus the relation $\tilde{\pi}$ must be reflexive, complete, and transitive, which is to say that it must be an ordering on Ω. Note that the derived relations π and $\sim$ are also transitive (though π is not reflexive and neither is complete).

We must make some assumptions further restricting the choice of relations. These may imply some loss of generality, and are made for simplicity. We then define a preference relation to be an ordering satisfying these assumptions.

Definition A preference relation $\tilde{\pi}$ is an ordering on Ω with the property that, for every x', the set
$$\{x \mid x\tilde{\pi}x'\}$$
is convex, contains every $x \geq x'$, and is closed, with
$$\{x \mid x'\tilde{\pi}x\}$$
also closed.

The set
$$\{x \mid x\tilde{\pi}x'\}$$
in this definition is the better set of x'. The assumption that this is closed is that of the continuity of the preference relation, in the sense that if every member of some sequence of consumptions is at least as preferred as a given consumption then the limit of the sequence has the same property. Together with the closedness of the corresponding worse set, this means that the indifference relation is also continuous, since the indifferent set
$$\{x \mid x \sim x'\}$$
is the intersection of two closed sets, and therefore closed. A further facet of this continuity which we shall use repeatedly is that if $x\pi\bar{x}$ then $x'\pi\bar{x}'$ for some x' and $\bar{x}'$ sufficiently close to x and $\bar{x}$ respectively. This assumption is not unreasonable, though it does rule out 'lexicographic preferences'. The assumption that the better set is convex requires that if any two (distinct) consumptions are weakly preferred to a third then any (proper) linear combination of these two is preferred to the third. This has two implications: firstly, it means that consumption is perfectly divisible, and secondly, it requires the consumer to prefer mixtures to extremes, or to have 'decreasing rates of substitution'. This is rather strong: weak convexity, which would permit 'perfect substitutes' would be more realistic. The assumption that the better set contain all larger consumptions is that of monotonicity, in the sense that all commodities are always desirable. Consider some $x \geq x'$, so that $x\tilde{\pi}x'$, and assume that $x \sim x'$; then by convexity
$$\bar{x} = (\tfrac{1}{2}x + \tfrac{1}{2}x')\pi x',$$

but $x' \geq \bar{x}$, which would require $x'\bar{\pi}\bar{x}$, a contradiction. Thus $x \geq x'$ implies the strong $x\pi x'$. Again this is rather strong, and the obvious weaker form would be more appropriate.

One should check that some ordering does in fact satisfy these assumptions, but this is straightforward. Then it is easy to see that the family of all indifferent sets defines a partition on Ω, and that, geometrically, each set is a 'hypersurface' convex from below; this is illustrated in Figure 2.1. In this interpretation it would

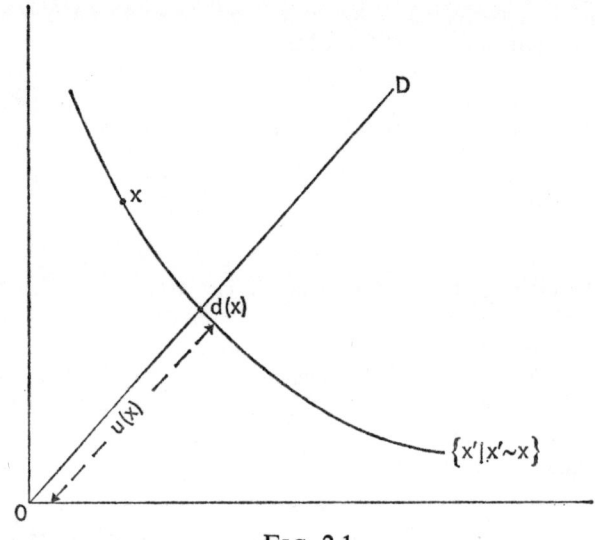

FIG. 2.1

be useful if we could represent preferences numerically, that is find some utility function assigning higher numbers to more preferred consumptions.

Definition A real-valued function u on Ω is a utility function for the preference ordering $\bar{\pi}$ if

$$u(x) \geqq u(x')$$

whenever $x\bar{\pi}x'$.

It would be more useful if we were able to represent preferences by a continuous utility function; this transpires to be possible.

Proposition 2.1 A preference ordering may be represented by a continuous utility function.

Proof Every x is indifferent to exactly one consumption, $d(x)$, on the diagonal of Ω, that is on

$$D = \{x \mid x = ae,\ a \geqq 0\}$$

(where e is the unit vector). The existence of $d(x)$ follows directly from completeness, monotonicity, and continuity, and its uniqueness from monotonicity. It is clear that

$$u(x) = \|d(x)\|$$

is a utility function. Now the continuity of $\sim$ implies that if $x^t \to x$ and $d(x^t) \to d'$ then $d' \sim x$; also, since D is closed, $d' \in D$. It follows that $d' = d(x)$, so that d is continuous. Since distance is continuous and

$$u(x) = \|d(x)\|$$

it follows that u is continuous.

The motivation behind this proof is straightforward: we need only assign utilities to indifferent sets, and this is done simply by measuring their distances (in the appropriate sense) from the worst, or zero, consumption. This is also illustrated in Figure 2.1. It is important to note that this concept of utility is simply a useful analytical tool, and has no higher metaphysical meaning. This is made clear by the observation that if u is a utility function then so is fu for any increasing function f. Also note that this proof does not use, and therefore does not require, convexity. However, if preferences are convex then it is clear that there will always be a quasi-concave utility function.

2.3 DEMAND

We have now determined the consumer's actions and preferences; all that remains is to specify what is available. To do this we suppose there is some price system p, and also, given this, that the consumer has some given income or wealth, say $a(p)$ units of account. Then a consumption x is available if its cost does not exceed the consumer's wealth, that is if $px \leq a$; however, because of monotonicity the consumer will not spend less than his wealth, so without loss of generality we may consider the consumptions available to be those whose cost equals the consumer's wealth, that is the set

$$\{x \mid px = a\}.$$

Geometrically, this is to say that the available set is a hyperplane in the commodity space.

We may now define the consumer's action, or demand; this is the most preferred consumption of those he can afford.

Definition The (individual) demand function $x(p)$ or $x(p, a(p))$ is defined by $x(p, a(p))$ is $\tilde{\pi}$-maximal on

$$\{x \mid px = a(p)\}.$$

We must of course ensure that such a function is well-defined, or that a unique maximum exists. Firstly, assume that prices are positive. Then the available set is closed and bounded (and non-empty). Now a $\tilde{\pi}$-maximum is equivalent to a maximum of u, which, given the continuity of u, is ensured by Weierstrass' theorem. Uniqueness is ensured by convexity: if x and x' were both maxima then

$$px = px' = a,$$

so, if

$$\bar{x} = \tfrac{1}{2}x + \tfrac{1}{2}x'$$

$p\bar{x} = a$ and $\bar{x}$ is available; but by convexity $\bar{x}\pi x \sim x'$, so x and x' could not be maxima. Now assume that $p_i = 0$ for $i \in S$ and $p_i > 0$ for $i \notin S$; then by monotonicity $x_i = \infty$ for $i \in S$, while the problem of choosing x_i for $i \notin S$ is simply the original problem with reduced dimensionality. Thus the demand function is defined in the regular sense on the positive orthant, and in the extended sense on the non-negative orthant. Geometrically, for positive prices, the demand is simply the unique point of tangency of the indifference hypersurface with the price hyperplane; this is illustrated in Figure 2.2.

An immediate property of the demand function which we shall use repeatedly is that any (other) consumption which is at least as preferred as the chosen consumption must cost more than the chosen consumption, that is

$$x'\tilde{\pi}x(p, a)$$

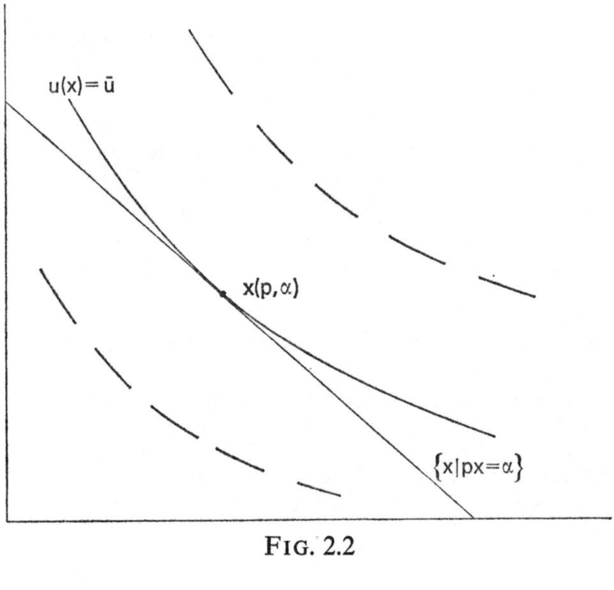

FIG. 2.2

(with $x' \neq x$) implies
$$px' > px(p, a).$$
This is related to the revealed preference property. Let (p, a) and (p', a') be two distinct price–income pairs, with
$$x = x(p, a),$$
$$x' = x(p', a')$$
and $x \neq x'$. Now if $px' \leq a$ then consumption x' is available under (p, a) but not chosen, so that x is revealed preferred to x'; but this means that x could not be available under (p', a'), or it would have been chosen, so that x' cannot be revealed preferred to x. Thus 'revealed preferred' is an asymmetric relation, or

implies
$$px' \leq px$$
$$p'x > p'x'.$$

A further property of the demand function is that it is homogeneous (of degree zero) in prices and income, that is
$$x(\lambda p, \lambda a) = x(p, a)$$
for any $\lambda > 0$. This follows directly from the definition.

The most important property of the demand function from the general equilibrium viewpoint is its continuity in prices (now treating wealth as a function of price). Not surprisingly, this requires wealth to be continuous, and in fact it also requires this to be positive.

Proposition 2.2 An individual demand function is continuous if wealth is continuous and positive.

Proof Let $p^t \to p$, so that
$$a(p^t) = a^t \to a > 0$$
and
$$x(p^t) = x^t \to x';$$
we must show that $x' = x(p)$. Firstly, $p^t x^t = a^t$, so $px' = a$. Now let $x'' \pi x'$, so that, for some $\lambda < 1$, $\lambda x'' \pi x'$ and thus $\lambda x'' \pi x^t$ for large t. This means that $\lambda p^t x'' > a^t$, so that $\lambda px'' \geq a$ and $px'' > a$. In other words x' is $\tilde{\pi}$-maximal on
$$\{x \mid px = a\},$$
or $x' = x(p)$.

It should be quite clear why we need the continuity of wealth. To see that we also need wealth to be positive, consider the example where $a(p) = p_1$, as would be the case if the real wealth or resources of the consumer consisted solely of one unit of commodity 1, and let $p^t \to \bar{p}$ where $\bar{p}_1 = 0$, so that $x^t \to 0$. Then for any positive price p^t the consumption of commodity 1 is bounded by wealth, so that $x_1(p^t) \leq 1$, but when $p_1 = 0$ this no longer applies, and by monotonicity $x_1(\bar{p}) = \infty$. Thus demand is not continuous at $\bar{p}$. The effect of this in the proof is that if $a = 0$ then $\lambda p x'' \geq a$ need not imply $px'' > a$.

It is useful to examine the effect of a change in prices on the chosen consumption. Consider specifically the effect of an increase in the price of some commodity with the prices of all other commodities and wealth unchanged. Clearly this cannot increase the consumer's utility level, and will in general decrease this. Similarly, an increase in wealth with all prices fixed must increase the consumer's utility level. Then because of continuity it is always possible to compensate the consumer for a price change by a wealth change of the same direction which leaves his utility level unchanged. We may therefore consider the effect of a price change as the sum of two effects: that of a compensated price change (the substitution effect), and that of the corresponding wealth change (the wealth effect).

Assume that some price increases, and consider first the wealth effect; note that this must be the effect of a decrease in wealth. Typically one would expect a decrease in wealth to bring about a decrease in consumption, so that the wealth effect would be negative; however, this is not necessarily so and may not apply for 'inferior' commodities. Now consider the substitution effect, specifically on the consumption of the commodity whose price has increased. If the two prices are p and p', and if $x = x(p)$ with $x' = x(p')$, then since $x \sim x'$ we must have

$$px < px',$$
$$p'x' < p'x;$$

rearranging these inequalities gives

$$(p - p')(x - x') < 0,$$

so that if $p'_i > p_i$ and $p'_j = p_j$ $(j \neq i)$ then $x'_i < x_i$. Thus the substitution effect is necessarily negative. It is then natural to expect the total effect to be negative, though this is still not necessary: if this is the case then the commodity is normal. Not surprisingly, at least one commodity must be normal, and all may be. These wealth (W) and substitution (S) effects are illustrated in Figure 2.3.

The effect of the change in price of one commodity on the demands for other commodities is also ambiguous, though, less definitely, we might expect a high price for one commodity to lead to switching from this commodity to others so these effects would be positive. If this does obtain for commodity i when the price of j changes then commodity i is a (gross) substitute for j; if not then commodity i is a (gross) complement for j. Note that commodity i may be a substitute for j, but j a complement for i. Also, at least one, and maybe all, other commodities must be substitutes for any given normal commodity. Further, the property of being normal, or a substitute or complement, is not intrinsic to the commodity and the consumer,

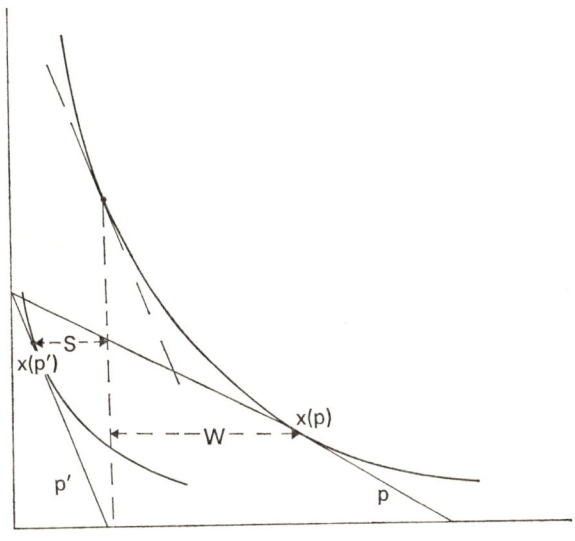

FIG. 2.3

but may depend on the price system. In Chapters 6 and 7 we concentrate on the canonical substitutes case, where all commodities are normal and all pairs of commodities are substitutes (at all prices).

2.4 PRODUCTION SETS

We now consider the second class of agents, that of producers. The discussion of producers' behaviour is less detailed than that of consumers for two reasons: firstly the formal structure, once established, is analogous to that for consumers; and secondly, for expository purposes, we always first consider the properties of exchange economies, where there are no producers, and only then extend the discussion to production economies.

The role of a producer is to choose a production plan, that is to specify exactly which commodities he will produce and which inputs to use in doing this. Such a plan may be represented by listing the outputs and inputs of the various commodities, designated $(y_1, \ldots y_n)$, or y. As a convention, inputs are treated as negative outputs so that, for example, if one unit of commodity 1 is produced from one unit of commodity 2 (and nothing else), we write

$$y = (1, -1, 0, \ldots 0).$$

Also, inputs and outputs are measured net, so if one unit of commodity 1 and one unit of commodity 2 are used to produce three units of commodity 1 we write

$$y = (2, -1, 0, \ldots 0).$$

Clearly a production is an element of the commodity space. This concept of production, as the parallel one of consumption, is quite wide: it includes transportation, since commodities are distinguished by location; and storage, since they are distinguished by date.

In parallel with the consumer, the producer chooses the most preferred action (or production) available to him. For the producer, however, the concept of preference is straightforward, but that of availability is correspondingly deeper. We commence with the latter.

The productions available to the producer do not depend on the price system, but are given by the technology, as perceived by the producer. In other words there is a given set of productions which are considered technologically feasible; this is his production set. Clearly a production set is a subset of the commodity space, but equally we could not reasonably interpret all such subsets as production sets. We must therefore make some assumptions restricting the choice of subsets we may interpret in this way; these assumptions define a production set.

Definition A production set Y is a closed, bounded above, convex subset of E containing every $y \leq 0$ and no $y \geq 0$.

The assumption of closedness is simply that of continuity, in the sense that if each member of a sequence of productions is feasible then so is its limit. This seems reasonable, though since zero production is feasible it does prohibit 'overhead costs'. The assumption that the production set be bounded above requires that outputs are limited, however large inputs become. This may be rather strong, but may not be very important in practice, since at any price system which will be of interest outputs will typically be below this bound anyway; also, it may be justified to some extent if we take account of the producer's 'entrepreneurship', which is fixed (but which is not a commodity since it is inalienable). The convexity assumption requires that any (proper) linear combination of two (distinct) feasible productions is feasible, even with wastage (that is, in the 'interior' of the production set). This has two implications: firstly, it means that production is perfectly divisible; and secondly, since zero production is feasible, it means that any fraction of a feasible production is possible, or in other words that decreasing returns to scale exist. This may be rather strong; weak convexity might be more realistic, since it would allow additivity (if two productions are individually feasible then they are jointly feasible). The assumptions that every non-positive and no semi-positive productions are feasible are straightforward. The first requires disposability, in the sense that one may have inputs with no outputs; together with convexity this implies free disposal, in that any production smaller than a feasible production is feasible. The second requires that there may be no free production, which is acceptable.

We should check that these assumptions are consistent, but this is trivial (for example $Y = \{0\}$ satisfies them). A typical production set is illustrated in Figure 2.4.

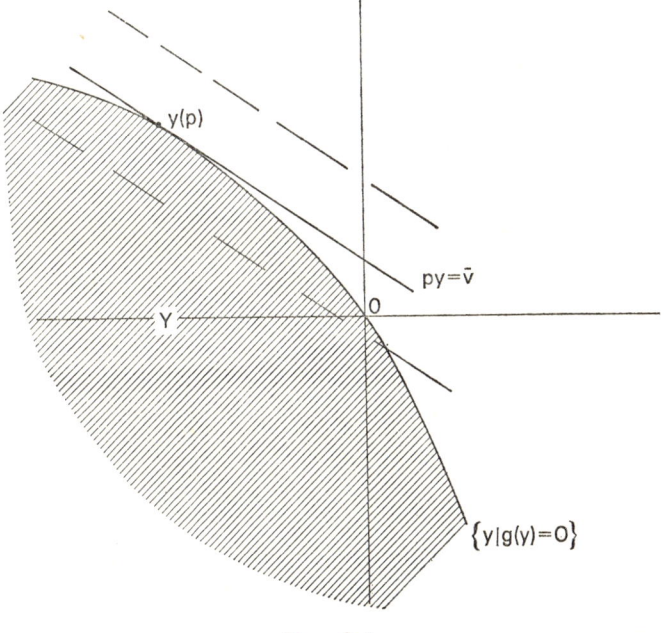

FIG. 2.4

2.5 SUPPLY

Now that we have determined the producer's actions and possibilities we need only specify his preferences. These are straightforward. Since all goodwill and future effects are implicitly taken account of in the definition of the commodities, the producer's preferences are defined by profit maximisation (relative to some given prices, p). Profit is simply the excess of revenue over costs, which, given the sign convention, is py. Thus a production y is preferred to y' if

$$py > py'.$$

We may now define the producer's action, or supply; this is the most profitable production of those which are feasible.

Definition The (individual) supply function $y(p)$ is defined by $py(p)$ maximises py on Y.

It is straightforward to show that this is well-defined, at least for positive prices. The available set is closed (and non-empty), and the function py is clearly continuous and bounded above, so a maximum exists. Uniqueness follows from convexity in the same way as for demand. If some prices are zero we must make a minor technical modification, but again we need only follow the argument for demand.

A production is 'efficient' if there is no larger feasible production. All such productions must be on the boundary of the production set, and therefore form (part of) a hypersurface in E concave from below. Since the set of productions yielding some given profit is a hyperplane in E, the supply chosen may be seen geometrically as the unique point of tangency of this hyperplane and hypersurface. This surface of efficient productions can be represented by

$$\{y \mid g(y) = 0\}$$

where g is some continuous quasi-convex function. This means that the producer's problem (for positive prices) may be seen as the maximisation of py subject to $g(y) = 0$, that is the maximisation of a linear function subject to a continuous quasi-convex constraint. This also is illustrated in Figure 2.4.

This may be compared with the consumer's problem, which may be seen as the maximisation of a continuous quasi-concave function ($u(x)$) subject to a linear constraint ($px = a$). Thus the producer's problem is a direct analogue of the dual of the consumer's (or vice versa). This makes the investigation of the properties of the supply function relatively straightforward.

It is at once clear that the supply function is homogeneous; this

follows directly from the definition. Also, it is continuous. Let $p^t \to p$ and
$$y(p^t) = y^t \to y';$$
then $y^t \in Y$, so that $y' \in Y$. Now for any $y'' \in Y$ we have
$$p^t y^t \geqq p^t y''$$
so that
$$py' \geqq py'',$$
which is to say that $y' = y(p)$. It follows that profit $py(p)$ is also continuous. Comparative static properties are simpler than those of demand, since there are no wealth effects. If there are two prices p and p', and if $y = y(p)$ with $y' = y(p')$, then we have
$$py > py',$$
$$p'y' > p'y;$$
thus
$$(p - p')(y - y') > 0.$$

Then if $p'_i > p_i$ and $p_j = p_j$ ($j \neq i$) we have $y'_i > y_i$, so that if the price of a commodity increases then its net output increases.

Notes

1 The general framework of commodities and prices follows that of G. Debreu [*Theory of Value*, New York, 1959], who discusses the distinction of commodities more fully; the question of ownership is treated in Chapter 5. The general theory of the behaviour of consumers and producers is from the core of standard microeconomics, though the discussion here concerns only those aspects of relevance to general equilibrium theory. A more complete treatment may be found in a standard microeconomics text, for example E. Malinvaud [*Lectures on Microeconomic Theory*, Amsterdam, 1972].

2 The axioms of preference may be relaxed somewhat. Monotonicity may be weakened to nonsatiation, that is every consumption has a more preferred consumption, but then the proof of the existence of a utility function is more complicated. Convexity can be weakened to weak convexity (in the obvious sense), but this destroys the uniqueness of the demand function, which is particularly important, since we must then work with correspondences rather than (point-valued) functions and of course require the associated new continuity concepts. The choice of consumptions may also be restricted to some (non-empty) closed

convex subset of Ω, because of 'biological feasibility'. For these various extensions see Debreu (and Problem 5).

3 The simple proof of the existence of a utility function follows Y. Kannai [Continuity Properties of the Core of a Market, *Econometrica*, 1970]. The attempt to extend this to the non-monotone case by K. J. Arrow and F. H. Hahn [*General Competitive Analysis*, San Francisco, 1971] is incorrect, though may be modified.

4 The production axioms may also be weakened. Convexity is required only in the weak form, but again uniqueness is destroyed and correspondences are required. Boundedness may be relaxed altogether for some purposes, though this has the effect of making production undefined at various (positive) prices. This is done by Debreu.

Problems

1 Show that the 'lexicographic preference relation' for two commodities defined by $x\pi y$ if (a) $x_1 > x_1'$ or (b) $x_1 = x_1'$ and $x_2 > x_2'$, is not continuous.

2 Specify a preference relation on Ω. Also show that the 'Cobb-Douglas' relation on Ω_+ defined by $x\pi x'$ if
$$x_1 \ldots x_n > x_1' \ldots x_n'$$
satisfies the preference axioms.

4 Show that a utility function is quasi-concave.

5 Show that a demand function is well-defined and continuous if consumption is restricted to some closed convex subset of Ω which contains some affordable consumption.

6 Show that at least one commodity must be normal, and all may be, and that at least one other commodity must be a substitute for any given commodity, and all may be.

7 Show that the maximum of profit on a production set is unique.

8 Show that, under a trivial modification, the supply function is well-defined when some prices are zero.

9 Show that production is irreversible, in that the negative of any (non-zero) feasible production is not feasible.

10 Show that the function g defining the set of efficient productions,
$$\{y \mid g(y) = 0\}$$
is continuous and quasi-convex.

3 Competitive Equilibrium

Now that we have a theory of the behaviour of the various agents as individuals, we may begin to study their interaction, which is the essence of general equilibrium theory. In this chapter we do this in the competitive framework, where we are able to demonstrate two of the three perhaps deepest propositions in economic theory: that the independent behaviour of a myriad of agents connected only by a price system can be consistent, and that the outcome of this is in some sense most desirable. (The third proposition must await Chapter 5.) We commence with the first question in the more simple context of an exchange economy, then consider some properties of the outcome of this, including the second question; finally, the whole discussion is extended to production.

3.1 CONCEPTS

The main question we consider is whether there exists a price system at which all the demands of the agents are consistent, in that in aggregate they balance resources. The question is relevant at two levels. Normatively, it asks whether the 'invisible hand' conjectured by Adam Smith does in fact operate, that is whether laisser-faire is at least possible. Positively, meaningful predictions in economics tend to concern equilibrium levels (if the harvest fails, the price of corn increases); a condition for such questions even to make sense therefore is that such levels exist.

We consider m consumers, indexed by $h = 1, \ldots m$. All attributes of agent h are identified by the corresponding superscript (though since two consumptions x^h and x'^h of consumer h will only be compared by this consumer, we typically omit the identification h from the preference relations $\tilde{\pi}^h$, π^h and $\sim^h$, and thus write $x^h \tilde{\pi}^h x'^h$ as $x^h \tilde{\pi} x'^h$, for example). Each consumer behaves as the individual consumer of Chapter 2, but with the additional specification that wealth is determined solely by the ownership of resources. Consumer h is endowed with non-negative amounts of the various commodities (with a positive amount of some), denoted $r^h = (r_1^h, \ldots r_n^h)$; thus at some price system p his wealth is the value of these, pr^h. His demand $x^h(p)$ is determed by the maximisation of his preferences on

$$\{x^h | px^h = pr^h\}.$$

Aggregate demand is the sum of these individual demands, denoted

$$x = \sum_h x^h,$$

and similarly aggregate resources are

$$r = \sum_h r^h;$$

their difference,

$$z = x - r$$

is excess demand.

An economy is defined by the attributes (preferences and resources) of its various consumers, that is by each $\tilde{\pi}^h$ and r^h. Formally, then an economy is the pair (Π, R), where Π is an array of preferences $(\tilde{\pi}^1, \ldots \tilde{\pi}^m)$ and R an array of resources $(r^1, \ldots r^m)$. The economy is in equilibrium if demands balance resources, that is if excess demand is zero. The price at which this occurs is an equilibrium price, and the resulting allocation of consumptions $X = (x^1, \ldots x^m)$ is an equilibrium allocation. The pair consisting of an equilibrium price and an equilibrium allocation is a competitive equilibrium, though loosely either of its components may be referred to as an equilibrium.

Definition The pair (p, X) is a competitive equilibrium of the economy (Π, R) if $x^h(p)$ is $\tilde{\pi}^h$-maximal on

$$\{x^h | px^h = pr^h\}$$

for each h and $x(p) = r$.

This concept is static, in that it does not involve any laws of movement, so is not necessarily relevant to the existence of equilibrium from the positive, or operational, viewpoint, though clearly it is what is required from the normative, or consistency, view. A technical objection to this definition is that we should consider demands and resources to be consistent even if the demand for some commodity with zero price (air) were less than its resource. However, since each demand is infinite at zero price and resources are finite such a state could not arise, so we may retain this simple definition. Note that we have shown that any equilibrium price must be positive.

Mathematically, an equilibrium is a possible solution to a number of real equations
$$(z_1 = 0, \ldots z_n = 0)$$

in a number of (real) variables $(p_1, \ldots p_n)$. It is of some interest then to count these equations and variables, though of course an equality between the numbers of these is neither necessary nor sufficient for the existence of a solution, let alone a meaningful solution with prices positive. There appear to be n variables, but in effect the homogeneity of the functions $x^h(p)$, discussed in Chapter 2, and thus of $x(p)$, means that there are only $n-1$ independent variables. This is because we may always replace $(p_1, \ldots p_n)$ by, say,

$$(p_1/p_n, \ldots p_{n-1}/p_n, 1),$$

provided that $p_n > 0$, without affecting the value of $x(p)$, which leaves only the $n-1$ relative prices

$$(p_1/p_n, \ldots p_{n-1}/p_n).$$

Similarly, there appear to be n equations, but in fact only $n-1$ of these are independent. This is because of the important proposition known as Walras' law: $pz(p) = 0$ for any p. This follows directly from adding the various constraints

$$px^h = pr^h,$$

which of course each $x^h(p)$ satisfies, to obtain

$$px = pr,$$

or $pz(p) = 0$. The essence of the economy is then given by these $n-1$ real equations in $n-1$ variables, which are embedded in the excess demand function z.

It is clear that the properties of the excess demand function determine the existence of an equilibrium. We have already noted that this obeys Walras' law, and that the aggregate demand function, and therefore this excess demand function, are homogeneous. Continuity follows from the continuity of the individual demand functions, at least when all endowments are positive.

Proposition 3.1 The excess demand function of a positively endowed economy is continuous.

Proof On the assumption that each $r^h > 0$, each wealth pr^h is positive and continuous at any $p \geq 0$. It follows from Proposition 2.2 that each x^h is continuous, as therefore are x, and

$$z = x - r.$$

Note that we need not consider all prices being zero. Also, excess demand may well be continuous even though some r^h is not positive, or equivalently will always be positive at positive prices (since then wealth is positive for any $r^h \geq 0$).

3.2 EXISTENCE

We demonstrate the existence of an equilibrium using the various properties of the excess demand function which we have established: continuity, homogeneity, Walras' law, and positive excess demand at zero price. Before examining the general case it is helpful to consider a simple two-commodity economy. Here we need only consider a single (real) equation: because of homogeneity we may fix $p_2 = 1$, say, and only consider variations in the normalised price p_1; because of Walras' law, z_2 will be zero if z_1 is zero, so we need only consider the value of z_1. Clearly p_1 is an equilibrium if

$$z_1(p_1, 1) = 0.$$

The reason why this will hold at some p_1 is straightforward. When price is zero demand is infinite, and thus excess demand is positive (in fact infinite too). On the other hand when price tends to infinity it is not difficult to see that excess demand is negative. Because excess demand is continuous, there must be some intermediary price where excess demand is zero. This is illustrated in Figure 3.1, where $\bar{p}_1$ is an equilibrium, as is any p_1 in the set S.

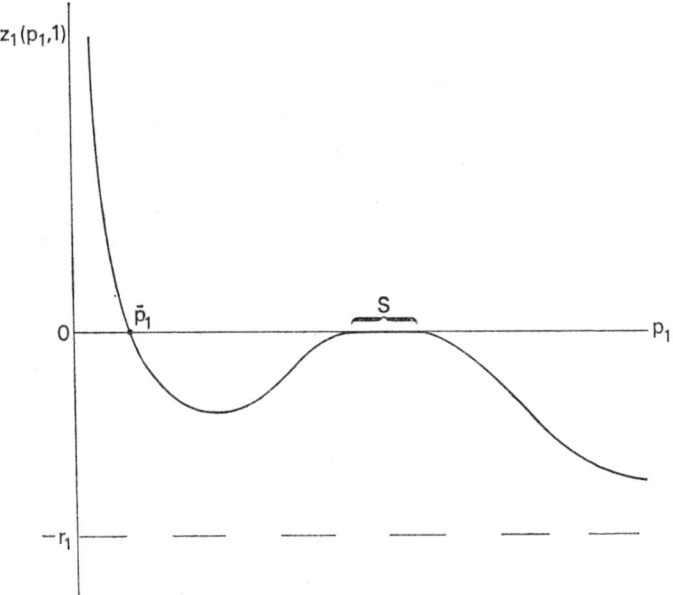

FIG. 3.1

COMPETITIVE EQUILIBRIUM

The approach in the general case is similar. We first use homogeneity to restrict our attention to normalised prices, though to avoid any problems caused by the possibility of free commodities prices are normalised so that they sum to unity. We then define some appropriate continuous function from the set of these admissible prices, the unit simplex, into itself, and observe that there is some point which is mapped onto itself. Finally, Walras' law is used to identify this fixed point with an equilibrium.

Proposition 3.2 A positively endowed economy has a competitive equilibrium.

Proof On the unit simplex Q_1 define

$$g_i(p) = 1 - 1/(1 + \max \{z_i(p), 0\}) \quad (i = 1, \ldots n)$$

(for $p > 0$, with $g_i(p) = 1$ whenever $p_i = 0$) and

$$f(p) = \frac{p + g(p)}{1 + g(p)e}.$$

Clearly f and g are both well-defined, and are continuous since z is continuous from Proposition 3.1; also, f maps from Q_1 to Q_1, since $pe = 1$ on Q_1. It follows from Brouwer's theorem that f has a fixed point, say $\bar{p}$. Then by definition

$$\bar{p}(1 + ge) = \bar{p} + g,$$

so that

$$gz = (ge)\bar{p}z = 0$$

(using Walras' law). But from the definition of g, $g_i z_i \geq 0$ for each i, so we can only have $g_i z_i = 0$ for each i. However, if $z_i > 0$ we must have $g_i > 0$ so $g_i z_i > 0$; thus $z \leq 0$. But then by Walras' law if $z_i < 0$ we must have $\bar{p}_i = 0$, which would imply $z_i = \infty$; thus $z \geq 0$. It follows that $z = 0$, so that $\bar{p}$ is an equilibrium.

The mapping used in the proof is defined in two parts. Firstly, the g_i map from all possible excess demands to the unit interval in a continuous way, such continuity depending on that of the z_i; they also have the property that $g_i = 0$ when $z_i = 0$. Secondly, f simply adds p to g, so that $f(p) = p$ when $z(p) = 0$, and then normalises so that $fe = 1$ and the range of f is contained in Q_1; again continuity is preserved. This mapping approximates the type of adjustment which one might expect actually to occur in the economy: the price of a commodity is raised if it has positive excess demand, and lowered if it has negative excess demand; this is related to the discussion of stability in Chapter 6.

Again, positive endowments are not necessary for the existence of an equilibrium. Indeed, it should be noted that these are only required to ensure the continuity of excess demands, but that these are automatically continuous at positive prices, and only a positive price could be an equilibrium!

It is sometimes simpler to interpret prices as being in terms of some given numeraire commodity (gold) rather than in abstract units of account. Then if p is any abstract price system the corresponding numeraire price system with numeraire n, say, is

$$(p_1/p_n, \ldots p_{n-1}/p_n, 1).$$

It is straightforward to show that a numeraire equilibrium exists.

Proposition 3.3 A positively endowed economy has a competitive numeraire equilibrium.

Proof We must show that, for some i, there exists an equilibrium price p with $p_i = 1$. If $\bar{p}$ is the equilibrium of Proposition 3.2 then $\bar{p} > 0$, since if $\bar{p}_i = 0$ we would have $z_i = \infty$. We may therefore define $p = \bar{p}/\bar{p}_i$: by homogeneity

$$z(p) = z(\bar{p}) = 0$$

so that p is an equilibrium, and clearly $p_i = 1$.

This is illustrated in Figure 3.2 (where $i = 2$). In view of this we will now interpret all prices as numeraire prices with numeraire n.

3.3 OPTIMALITY

We now consider the second of the three basic questions: to what extent is the equilibrium optimal. To do this we must first define

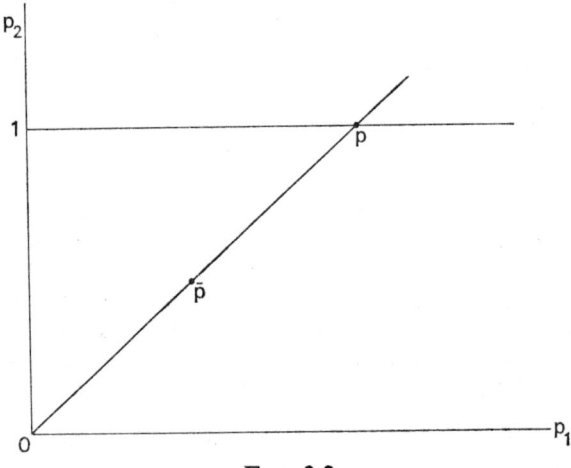

FIG. 3.2

COMPETITIVE EQUILIBRIUM

when an equilibrium, or more specifically, an equilibrium allocation, is optimal. If at least one consumer, h say, prefers an allocation X to an alternative X', in the sense that $x^h \, \pi \, x'^h$, and no consumer prefers X' to X, then X is socially preferred to X'. Not all allocations are feasible: an allocation is only feasible if aggregate consumption does not exceed total resources. Accordingly, we define an allocation to be an optimum if there is no socially preferred feasible allocation.

Definition The allocation X is an optimum of the economy (Π, R) if $x'^h \, \tilde{\pi} \, x^h$ for each h with strict preference for some implies that $x'_i > r_i$ for some i.

This Paretian concept of optimality is weak in that there may be many optima, none of which are comparable in this sense, yet which have different evaluations according to other criteria, such as equity. However, the converse of this weakness is that a non-optimal state is certainly to be avoided. Of course we may always strengthen the social preference relation on which this is based by specifying that two allocations are socially indifferent unless one is socially preferred; the value judgements underlying these normative interpretations are discussed in the Appendix.

We ask whether an equilibrium is necessarily an optimum, and conversely. Remarkably, both answers (subject to a minor qualification) are in the affirmative: all individuals independently pursuing their own ends not only produce order rather than chaos, but also produce a 'best' allocation, and any 'best' allocation may be generated as a competitive outcome.

The first result says that no allocation socially preferable to the equilibrium can be achieved. The demonstration of this is straightforward, simply noting that an improvement costs more.

Proposition 3.4 A competitive equilibrium is an optimum.

Proof We must show that if $(p, \bar{X})$ is an equilibrium of (Π, R) then $\bar{X}$ is an optimum. Now if $x^h \, \tilde{\pi} \, \bar{x}^h$ for each h with strict preference for some $(h = k)$ then

$$px^h \geqq p\bar{x}^h$$

for each h with inequality for $h = k$, so that

$$px > p\bar{x} = pr,$$

and therefore $x_i > r_i$ for some i.

The second result, which is of more operational interest, says that whatever optimal state X may be chosen (for equity), this may be obtained in a decentralised way for some distribution of the available resources (namely X itself). In other words, if the appropriate redistribution of resources were made there would be an equilibrium price at which there was no trade, so that this redistribution was retained. This explains the theorem: under an optimal distribution of resources any trade would decrease some individual's utility and therefore would not be made, so that there is an equilibrium. It also explains the necessary qualification that each individual has a positive consumption at the optimum. The demonstration of this is not quite as straightforward, and is best interpreted geometrically. We consider the set (S) of all trades, that is individual consumptions less resources, which could produce an allocation as socially desirable as the optimum $(\bar{X})$, and note that this is convex and contains no negative vectors. We then use Minkowski's theorem to draw a hyperplane through the origin bounding this set, the normal (p) to which corresponds to an equilibrium price supporting the optimum. This is illustrated in Figure 3.3.

Proposition 3.5 A positive optimum may be obtained as a competitive equilibrium.

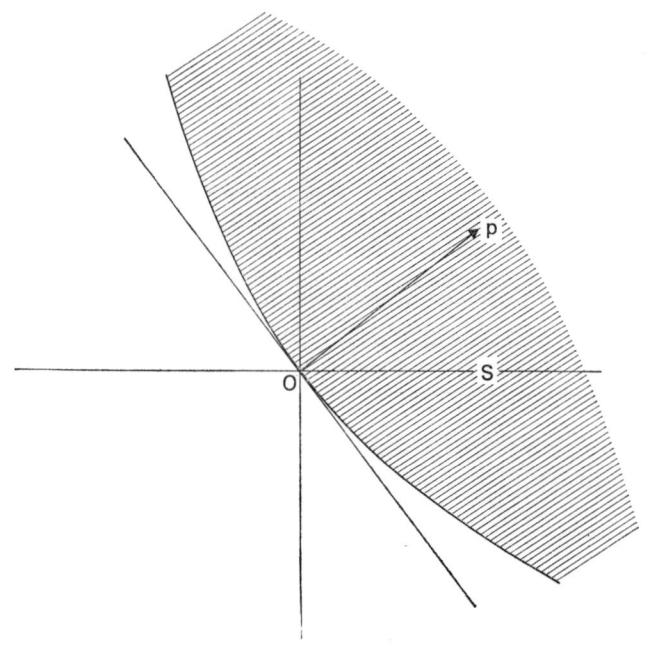

Fig. 3.3

Proof We must show that if $\bar{X}$ is an optimum of (Π, R) with each $\bar{x}^h > 0$ then, for some p, $(p, \bar{X})$ is an equilibrium of $(\Pi, \bar{X})$; note that $\bar{x} = r$ so that $(\Pi, \bar{X})$ is obtained from (Π, R) simply by redistributing resources. Let

$$S = \{x = \Sigma_h x^h | x^h \,\tilde{\pi}\, \bar{x}^h \text{ for each } h\}$$

be the set of 'weakly better' consumptions and, for some fixed k,

$$T = \{z = x - r | x \in S, x^k \,\pi\, \bar{x}^k\}$$

the set of 'better' trades. Convexity of preferences implies that T is convex. Further, T contains no $z < 0$, for otherwise there would be some corresponding element of S,

$$x = z + r < r,$$

with $x^k \,\pi\, \bar{x}^k$; but then the associated allocation X would be feasible and socially preferred to $\bar{X}$, contradicting the optimality of $\bar{X}$. Then by Minkowski's theorem there is some $p \geq 0$ such that $pz \geqq 0$ for every $z \in T$, or equivalently

$$px \geqq pr$$

for every $x \in S$ with $x^k \,\pi\, \bar{x}^k$. But in fact this holds even if $x^k \sim \bar{x}^k$, for then

$$x^k(\lambda) = (\lambda x^k + (1 - \lambda) x'^k) \,\pi\, \bar{x}^k$$

when $x'^k \,\tilde{\pi}\, x^k$ and $0 < \lambda < 1$ (by convexity), so that the inequality $px \geqq pr$ continues to hold when x^k is replaced by $x^k(\lambda)$, as it does in the limit as $\lambda \to 1$, when

$$x^k(\lambda) = x^k \sim \bar{x}^k.$$

We have then

$$px \geqq pr = p\bar{x}$$

for every $x \in S$. Setting $x^h = \bar{x}^h$ for $h \neq j$ this gives, for any j,

$$px^j \geqq p\bar{x}^j$$

for every $x^j \,\tilde{\pi}\, \bar{x}^j$, so that $\bar{x}^j$ minimises cost, subject to achieving the given utility. Finally, if

$$px^j \leqq p\bar{x}^j$$

then

$$p\lambda x^j < p\bar{x}^j$$

when $0 < \lambda < 1$ so that, as $\bar{x}_j$ minimises cost, $\bar{x}^j \,\pi\, \lambda x^j$; thus in the limit as $\lambda \to 1$, $\bar{x}^j \,\tilde{\pi}\, x^j$, and $\bar{x}^j$ maximises utility, subject to the given cost. It follows that $(p, \bar{X})$ is an equilibrium.

Note that we still have the cost-minimising property of the

optimum if we relax the requirement that all resources be positive. In fact it is not difficult to see that we will typically retain the preference-maximising property, and thus the competitive equilibrium, without this requirement, though not invariably.

3.4. UNIQUENESS

A further possible property of the equilibrium is its uniqueness. This is of obvious operational relevance, for if we are to compare equilibria we must know which equilibria to examine. It is also of interest as an indication of the determinateness of the invisible hand. The uniqueness referred to is that of the numeraire equilibrium price; because of homogeneity the abstract price system could only be unique up to a multiple. If the numeraire equilibrium price is unique then clearly the equilibrium allocation is unique, so we refer to the equilibrium as being unique.

It is apparent that equilibrium will not be unique if no further restrictions are made. This is suggested by the two-commodity example illustrated in Figure 3.1, where there are infinitely many equilibria. It is not difficult to specify an economy with multiple equilibria: all that is required is that excess demand decreases until becoming negative and then increases again until becoming positive. This counterexample suggests that we would ensure uniqueness if we ensured that excess demand were monotone (decreasing), as in Figure 3.4, where $\bar{p}_1$ is the unique equilibrium; this is the approach we adopt in the general case.

We may, at the cost of some loss of information, define the economy by its excess demand system z, rather than by the more basic parameters (Π, R). In the following discussion (and elsewhere) it is more convenient to adopt this approach; we therefore refer to the economy as z or (Π, R) interchangeably. The restriction we apply to the economy z to ensure that, effectively, excess demands are monotone is that of substitutability, in the sense used in Chapter 2. The economy is substitutive if a rise in the price of some commodity leads to substitution into, that is an increase in the excess demand for, other commodities.

Definition The economy z is substitutive if $p_i > \bar{p}_i$ and $p_j = \bar{p}_j$ for each $j \neq i$ implies

$$z_j(p) > z_j(\bar{p}) \quad (j \neq i).$$

An equivalent condition, obtained by repetitive use of the definition, is that if $p_i \geq \bar{p}_i$ for each i with equality for each $i \in S$ and inequality for some $i \notin S$ then

$$z_i(p) > z_i(\bar{p})$$

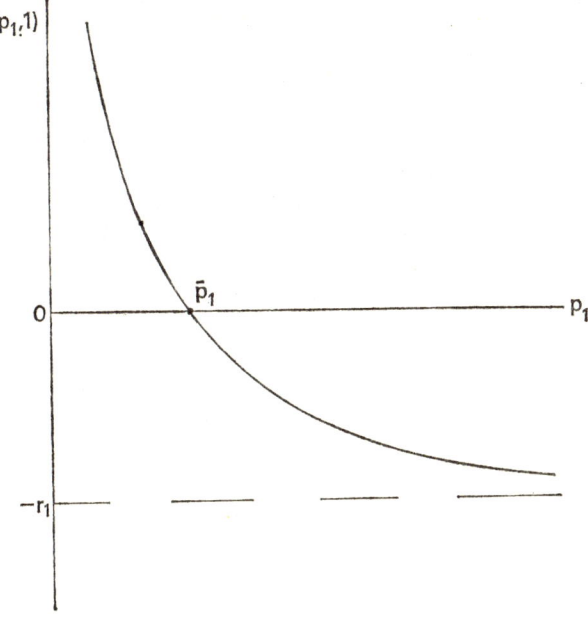

Fig. 3.4

for each $i \in S$. If this property applies then Walras' law implies that excess demand must fall when price rises, which gives the required monotonicity.

Although it is clear that many economies (with bread and butter as commodities) may not be substitutive, the commonness of substitutes suggested in Chapter 2 makes this case worth considering, at least as a canonical one from which to extend the theory. This property is also used in the later discussion of stability and comparative statics.

Proposition 3.6 The competitive equilibrium of a substitutive economy is unique.

Proof Let $\bar{p}$ be a numeraire equilibrium and for any $p \neq \bar{p}$ define
$$m = \max_i p_i/\bar{p}_i = p_k/\bar{p}_k$$
say, and $p' = m\bar{p}$. Then $p'_i \geqq p_i$ for each i with equality for $i = k$ and inequality for some $i \neq k$, so that by substitutability
$$z_k(p) < z_k(p').$$
But by homogeneity
$$z(p') = z(\bar{p}) = 0$$
so that $z_k(p) < 0$ and p is not an equilibrium.

Note that this proof shows that the excess demand for the commodity whose price is the largest, relative to the equilibrium price, is negative; in the same way it may be shown that the excess demand for the commodity with the lowest price is positive.

In the cases where equilibrium may not be unique it is of some interest to establish that various equilibria are in some sense connected, specifically that the set of equilibria is convex. This will be the case if the economy displays revealed preference. It was shown in Chapter 2 that individual demand functions had the revealed preference property, in that

implies
$$px^h(\bar{p}) \leqq px^h(p)$$

$$\bar{p}x^h(\bar{p}) < \bar{p}x^h(p)$$

for any distinct prices p and $\bar{p}$. However, this does not imply that aggregate demands, and therefore excess demands, necessarily have this property, though it suggests that they may typically: for example, it certainly holds if all consumers are identical. If this does hold then

implies
$$pz(\bar{p}) \leqq pz(p)$$

$$\bar{p}z(\bar{p}) < \bar{p}z(p),$$

so that if $\bar{p}$ is an equilibrium the antecedent becomes $pz(p) \geqq 0$, which is satisfied because of Walras' law, while the inevitable conclusion is $\bar{p}z(p) > 0$.

Definition The economy z displays revealed preference if $\bar{p}z(p) > 0$ whenever $z(\bar{p}) = 0$ and $z(p) \neq 0$.

Proposition 3.7 The set of competitive equilibrium prices of a revealed preference economy is convex.

Proof Let p and $\bar{p}$ be equilibrium prices and suppose that

$$p' = \lambda p + (1 - \lambda)\bar{p}$$

where $0 < \lambda < 1$, is not. Then $pz(p') > 0$ and $\bar{p}z(p') > 0$ so that $p'z(p') > 0$, which contradicts Walras' law.

3.5 PRODUCTION

It is straightforward to extend the discussion to a production economy. In addition to the consumers there are now l producers, indexed by $k = 1, \ldots, l$, all attributes of producer k being identified by the corresponding superscript. Thus, at the price system p, producer k chooses the production y^k which maximises his profit $v^k = py^k$ on his production set Y^k. These profits are owned by various consumers: consumer h owns a share s^{hk} of the profit of producer k (where each $s^{hk} \geq 0$ and each $\Sigma_h s^{hk} = 1$). Thus consumer h acts as above except that his wealth $a^h(p)$ is now $pr^h + vs^h$ rather than pr^h (where the vectors v and s^h are defined in the obvious way). Aggregate supply, y, which will be part positive and part negative, is total production $\Sigma_k y^k$; excess demand is the excess of demand over resources and supply,

$$z = x - r - y.$$

The economy is now defined by the various preferences and resources, together with the array of shares $S = (s^1, \ldots s^l)$, and the array of production sets $\Gamma = (Y^1, \ldots Y^l)$; again, this may equivalently be represented by the excess demand system. A price is an equilibrium price if the resulting excess demands are zero, while the triple consisting of an equilibrium price together with the corresponding allocation and production configuration $Y = (y^1, \ldots y^l)$ is an equilibrium.

The demonstration of the existence of equilibrium in Proposition 3.2 depends only on four properties of the excess demand function: continuity, homogeneity, Walras' law and positive excess demand at zero price. Firstly, it was shown in Chapter 2 that each production y^k is continuous; it follows that aggregate production y is continuous, as is each profit $v^k = py^k$. Also, aggregate demand x will be continuous exactly as in Proposition 3.1 provided that each wealth $pr^h + vs^h$ is continuous, which is clearly the case (since v is continuous). It follows that

$$z = x - r - y$$

is continuous in p. Secondly, it was shown in Chapter 2 that each y^k, and thus y, is homogeneous so that profits are proportional to prices:

$$v(\lambda p) = \lambda v(p)$$

for any $\lambda > 0$. This means that wealth, $pr^h + vs^h$, is still proportional to prices so that demand x, and therefore

$$z = x - r - y,$$

is still homogeneous. Thirdly, adding the various budget constraints

$$px^h = pr^h + vs^h$$

gives

$$px = pr + ve,$$

while adding the various profit definitions, $v^k = py^k$, gives

$$ve = py.$$

It follows that

$$pz = px - pr - py = 0$$

for all p, so that Walras' law still applies. Fourthly, demand is still infinite at zero price, while resources and production (outputs) are bounded, so that excess demand is certainly positive at zero price. Then since these four properties of the excess demand function ensure the existence of an equilibrium this is established for the production economy. The existence of a numeraire equilibrium follows from this exactly as in Proposition 3.3.

An allocation is an optimum if any socially preferable state X is unattainable, now in the sense that, for some i,

$$x_i > r_i + y_i$$

for all feasible y (those where $y^k \in Y^k$ for each k). Just as in Proposition 3.4, if an allocation X is socially preferred to an equilibrium allocation $\bar{X}$ then

$$px > p\bar{x} = pr + p\bar{y}$$

where p is the corresponding equilibrium price and $\bar{y} = y(p)$. Then, since $\bar{y}$ maximises profits,

$$py^k \leqq p\bar{y}^k$$

for all $y^k \in Y^k$, for each k, so that

$$py \leqq p\bar{y}.$$

It follows that

$$px > pr + py$$

and thus that, for some i,

$$x_i > r_i + y_i$$

for all feasible y. We have shown then that Proposition 3.4 carries over to production, and an equilibrium is an optimum. Proposition 3.5 also carries over with the appropriate changes: if $\bar{X}$ is an optimum for (Π, R, S, Γ) with each $\bar{x}^h > 0$ then, for some p, $(p, \bar{X}, Y(p))$ is an equilibrium for the same basic economy with the appropriate redistribution of resources and shares: for example

$$r^h = \bar{x}^h - y/m$$

(provided that each $\bar{x}^h > y/m$) and $s^h = e/m$. Thus if a particular optimum is chosen for reasons of equity, we could distribute resources in this way and distribute production and profits equally; the result would be an equilibrium. The demonstration of this is parallel to that of Proposition 3.5, only the set T is replaced by

$$\{z = x - r - y \,|\, x \in S,\ x^k\ \pi\ \bar{x}^k,\ y^j \in Y^j \text{ for each } j\}.$$

The uniqueness of equilibrium in Proposition 3.6, or the convexity of the equilibrium price set in Proposition 3.7, was established using

COMPETITIVE EQUILIBRIUM   41

only the properties of the excess demand functions which established existence with the added condition of substitutability, or revealed preference. It follows that both propositions carry over directly to the production economy, provided we interpret substitutability or revealed preference as applying to demand less supply rather than to demand. This seems neither more nor less restrictive for substitutability, though may be more restrictive for revealed preference.

Notes
1 The general framework of this chapter is that of L. Walras [*Elements of Pure Economics*, London, 1954 (Paris, 1874)]; the formal approach is closer to that of G. Debreu [*Theory of Value*, New York, 1959], where equivalent results are shown under the weaker conditions discussed in Notes 2 and 4 of Chapter 2, and existence is shown without the positive endowments requirement. It is clear that any economy (Π, R) has an associated excess demand function; it is helpful for counterexamples to note that the converse is true, that is that there is some economy (Π, R), in fact one consisting of n consumers, which generates any excess demand function for n commodities; this is shown by G. Debreu [Excess Demand Functions, *Journal of Mathematical Economics*, 1974].
2 Perhaps the most restrictive preference axiom is that of (strict or weak) convexity, for this both requires the consumer to be 'moderate' (preferring whisky and gin to all whisky) and prohibits any indivisibilities in consumption (as in cars). It is not difficult to see that existence cannot be ensured without convexity. However, one might expect that individual non-convexities would become unimportant in aggregate, so that there would be an approximate equilibrium, in some sense, in large economies; this is shown by R. M. Starr [Quasi-Equilibria in Markets with Nonconvex Preferences, *Econometrica*, 1969]. Alternatively, if the economy were very large, that is had uncountably many agents, one might expect individual non-convexities to have no importance in the aggregate, so that there would be an exact equilibrium; this is shown by R. J. Aumann [Existence of Competitive Equilibrium in Markets with a Continuum of Traders, *Econometrica*, 1966].
3 Most of the analysis of this chapter may be extended to the cases where the number of commodities or of agents is not finite. The importance of this extension for commodities is that, since commodities are dated, it allows us to consider the whole future, and not have some arbitrary horizon; this is discussed by B. Peleg and M. Yaari [Markets with Countably Many Commodi-

ties, *International Economic Review*, 1970], for example. For agents, this allows us to obtain a truly competitive economy, where each agent is of zero 'size', which is not possible in a finite economy: this is discussed by Aumann.

4 The condition of substitutability used to demonstrate uniqueness may be relaxed to weak substitutability (where the strict inequality in the definition is replaced by a weak inequality), provided that the economy remains connected in the sense that the commodities cannot be partitioned into two sets where the price of any member of the first does not affect the excess demand of some member of the second. There are also some alternative conditions, of which the most appealing is that of diagonal dominance, or that own price effects are more important than indirect effects (this is also used, and defined, in Chapter 6). In the case where excess demands are differentiable, which is required for this condition, diagonal dominance implies substitutability. These alternative conditions are discussed by K. J. Arrow and F. H. Hahn [*General Competitive Analysis*, San Francisco, 1971].

Problems

1 Compute the competitive equilibrium of the two-commodity two-consumer economy defined by

$$u^h(x^h) = x^h_1 x^h_2 \ (h = 1, 2),$$

$$R = ((1, 0), (0, 2)).$$

2 Show that the two-commodity two-consumer 'economy' defined by

$$u^1(x^1) = (x^1_1)^{1/2} (x^1_2)^{1/2}$$

$$u^2(x^2) = (x^2_1)^2 (x^2_2)^2$$

$$R = ((1, 0), (0, 1))$$

does not satisfy the preference requirements, and also that it has no equilibrium.

3 Show that the economy defined in Problem 1 is a substitutive revealed preference economy.

4 Demonstrate why an optimum which is not positive need not be an equilibrium.

5 Show that Proposition 3.2 continues to apply if each consumer's demand is restricted to some closed convex subset of Ω which contains his resources.

6 Show that in a substitutive economy all commodities are normal,

and that whose price is the smallest, relative to the equilibrium price, is positive.
7 Show that an exchange economy where all consumers are identical displays revealed preference.
8 Construct an economy (Π, R) which does not display revealed preference.
9 Construct an economy z with two equilibria (so that the set of equilibrium prices is not convex), and also an economy which is not substitutive yet has a unique equilibrium.
10 Complete the demonstration that a positive optimum is an equilibrium in a production economy.

4 Co-operative Equilibrium

Chapter 3 considered the existence of an equilibrium as a state at which a competitive economy would be in balance when individual agents acted independently, and were only related to each other through the price system. The present chapter considers what may be regarded as a more fundamental question: in what sense is there an equilibrium for the economy when agents may co-operate with each other in any way, and where there is no explicit concept of price? We thus demonstrate the third of the three propositions referred to in Chapter 3: that, in the limit as the number of agents grows, the equilibrium state allowing any manner of co-operation and not using a price system coincides with the price-based competitive equilibrium. Again, we first consider the exchange economy, and then incorporate production.

4.1 EDGEWORTH BOX

It is helpful to consider a simple geometric representation known as the Edgeworth Box; this is illustrated in Figure 4.1. We consider a two-commodity two-consumer economy where each consumer's preferences are 'smooth', and the total resource of each commodity is one unit. Since any feasible allocation X is characterised by having $x = e$, we may represent such a state by a point in a unit square, the Edgeworth Box. In figure, O^I is the origin of the commodity space of the first consumer (labelled I), and O^{II} that for the second (labelled II). The horizontal distance of a point X from the point O^I, which will be written as $|O^I \, X|_1$, measures I's consumption of commodity one in the state X, that is x_1^I, while $|O^{II} \, X|_1$ measures x_1^{II}; clearly these two horizontal distances sum to unity, as required. Similarly the vertical distance $|O^I \, X|_2$ measure x_2^I, and $|O^{II} \, X|_2$ measures x_2^{II}.

We may represent preferences by their associated indifference classes, or indifference curves. In the figure, those for I are the solid curves convex to O^I, and those for II the broken curves convex to O^{II}. Now consider the point A: clearly this does not represent an optimal state, since the point E (for example) lies on an indifference curve further from the relevant origin for both consumers, and is therefore preferred by both. On the other hand, E does represent an optimum, since any change must harm at least one consumer; similarly B and C (and also O^I and O^{II}) are optima. We see then that the set of optima consists of those points where the two consumers' indifference curves are tangential (together with some of the boundary

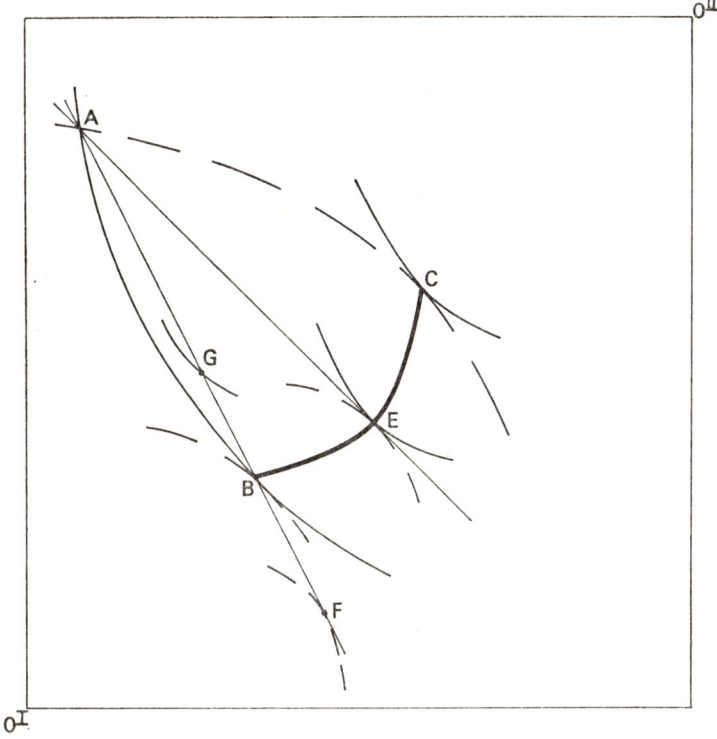

Fig. 4.1

of the box); it is not difficult to see that this is a continuous curve (a part of which is shown as the heavy curve in the figure).

Given some initial resources the consumers may co-operate to achieve some new allocation: this of course is by trading with each other. The basic question is which allocations would emerge as result of such trading, or which allocations could be considered a co-operative equilibria. Clearly an allocation will only be an equilibrium in this sense if neither consumer can do better than it either unilaterally or in conjunction with the other. Specifically, this means that an equilibrium must be no worse than the initial state for each consumer, and also be an optimum: the set of these allocations, or equilibria, is the core of the economy. If initial resources are represented by the point A then the core of the economy will consist of those optima which are no worse than A for I or for II; this is the set of points on the heavy curve in the figure. From this construction it is straightforward to show that the economy will always have a core, or that the core is non-empty, but that unless the initial allocation itself is an optimum there will be (infinitely) many allocations in the core.

It is constructive to look at the competitive equilibrium in this framework. Such a state is characterised by a price vector, with each consumer maximising his preferences subject to the budget constraint implied by these prices. In the case considered here this means that (provided the consumer consumes both commodities) his consumption is at the point of tangency of some indifference curve and the budget line. Since the price vector is common to both consumers this in turn means that both indifference curves are tangential to each other, which illustrates that the competitive equilibrium is an optimum (Proposition 3.4).

A positive price vector p may be represented in the figure by a line with a slope of p_1/p_2 (with respect to either origin), and will act as a budget constraint for both consumers if both their initial resources lie on it, that is if it passes through the point A (as does the line AE). It is not difficult to show that in fact there is some line passing through A which is of the same slope as the common indifference curve slope at the point where it meets the core (E in the figure), and thus that there is a competitive equilibrium. In this case the equilibrium price vector is

$$(|AE|_2, |AE|_1)$$

(or some multiple of this). But this is only an illustration of Proposition 3.2; of more interest is the result that the competitive equilibrium is in the core. A further point illustrated here is that we may draw a price line tangential to both indifference curves at any optimum point, so that any optimum is attainable as a competitive equilibrium (Proposition 3.5).

4.2 THE CORE

These ideas may be extended to economies with arbitrary numbers of commodities and consumers. There is no problem in extending the number of commodities, providing we do not want to represent the analysis geometrically; the interesting extension is of the number of consumers. Once we have more than two consumers we must allow for the possibility of some of these coming together and trading only amongst themselves. Consider for example the two-commodity three-consumer economy where preferences and resources are defined by

$$u^h(x^h) = x_1^h x_2^h \quad (h = 1, \ldots 3),$$
$$R = ((4, 4), (4, 4), (0, 8)).$$

For this economy it is clear that, compared with the initial allocation R, each individual prefers the allocation

$$X = ((4, 8), (3, 6), (1, 2)),$$

and also that this is an optimum. However, we would not expect such an allocation to prevail, for if individuals 2 and 3 form a coalition and only trade with each other, they could obtain the allocation

$$X' = ((4, 4), (3, 8), (1, 4))$$

which is preferred by each of these two consumers. In this case the allocation X' dominates X (through the coalition consisting of individuals 2 and 3).

More generally, a coalition is a (non-empty) subset of the set M of consumers. An allocation X dominates X' if there is a coalition which socially prefers X to X' and can actually achieve X by trading within itself; such a coalition blocks X'. An allocation is then a co-operative equilibrium if it is not dominated, and it is feasible; equivalently, the core is the set of undominated feasible allocations. (We may note here an analogy with the theory of games, for the economy becomes an m-person co-operative game, and the core of the economy is precisely the core of game theory).

Definition An allocation X is a co-operative equilibrium of the economy (Π, R) if, for all coalitions S, $x'^h \tilde{\pi} x^h$ for each $h \in S$ with strict preference for some implies that

$$\Sigma_S x_i^h > \Sigma_S r_i^h$$

for some i.

Note that a co-operative equilibrium must not be dominated by any coalition S, including $S = M$ and $S = \{h\}$. The first case immediately implies that a co-operative equilibrium is an optimum, while the second implies that for each consumer it is preferable to his resources. This core is then a proper generalisation of the core in the two-consumer case: we have retained 'group' and 'individual rationality', and added 'coalition rationality'. Also note that in principle we could have X dominating X' and vice versa, which could mean that there was no undominated allocation.

Since a competitive equilibrium is an optimum, and many optima are in the core (refer to the heavy curve in the figure), we might expect all competitive equilibrium to be in the core. This may be shown in exactly the same way as it was shown that a competitive equilibrium was an optimum (Proposition 3.4).

Proposition 4.1 A competitive equilibrium is a co-operative equilibrium.

Proof We must show that if $(p, \bar{X})$ is a competitive equilibrium of (Π, R) then $\bar{X}$ is a co-operative equilibrium. Now if, for some coalition S, $x^h \tilde{\pi} \bar{x}^h$ for each $h \in S$ with strict preference for some $(h = k)$ then

$$px^h \geqq p\bar{x}^h$$

for each $h \in S$ with strict inequality for $h = k$, so that

$$p\Sigma_S x^h > p\Sigma_S \bar{x}^h = p\Sigma_S r^h$$

and therefore

$$\Sigma_S x_i^h > \Sigma_S r_i^h$$

for some i.

Since Proposition 3.2 assures the existence of a competitive equilibrium a corollary to this proposition is that there exists a co-operative equilibrium, or that the core is non-empty. Indeed, not only is it non-empty, but it typically contains infinitely many elements, so the co-operative equilibrium is not unique, even when the competitive equilibrium is. This follows for example from the figure, where the unique competitive equilibrium is the point E, but the core contains all the points on the heavy curve.

4.3 ASYMPTOTIC CORE

In a finite economy each individual's exchanges have a finite effect on aggregate excess demands and thus on prices, so that perfect competition, in the sense of these effects being infinitesimal, cannot prevail. Since consumers will take advantage of these effects many co-operative equilibria will differ from the competitive equilibria. However, one might expect these differences to be smaller in larger economies, since then each individual's 'weight' is smaller, and to disappear in the limit (in some sense). To examine this question we must define the concept of an economy growing, and of the limit of such a process. Since we are concerned with the characteristics of some given finite economy, we must let this grow in a way which maintains these characteristics. This is by replication, that is adding a new agent identical to each existing agent. Specifically, given an economy (Π, R) with m consumers, we define an economy with $2m$

consumers, the first two (of type 1) having the characteristics $(\bar{\pi}^1, r^1)$, the second two (of type 2) the characteristics $(\bar{\pi}^2, r^2)$, and so on; this economy is represented by $(\Pi, R)^2$.

Consider the core of the replicated economy $(\Pi, R)^2$, where (Π, R) is the example illustrated in the figure. If we write the allocation X as

$$(x^{I1}, x^{I2}, x^{II1}, x^{II2})$$

then it is clear that we must have $x^{I1} = x^{I2}$ and $x^{II1} = x^{II2}$ when X is in the core, for otherwise X would be dominated by

$$(x^I, x^I, x^{II}, x^{II})$$

where

$$x^I = \tfrac{1}{2}(x^{I1} + x^{I2})$$

and x^{II} is defined similarly. This means that we may continue to represent the core on only two axes, or in the Edgeworth Box of the figure, and thus compare the cores of the two economies. It is obvious that the core of $(\Pi, R)^2$ is no larger than that of (Π, R), for any coalition which can block in the latter can certainly block in the former. In fact the core of the larger economy is actually smaller. In the figure, the whole of the heavy curve joining B and C, including the endpoints, is the core of (Π, R): however, the endpoint B, for example, is not in the core of $(\Pi, R)^2$. To see this, consider the coalition consisting of both consumers of type I and one of type II. Instead of accepting the trade B the type-II consumer could exchange $|AF|_1$ units of the first commodity for $|AF|_2$ of the second with each type-I consumer in equal shares, so that each type-I consumer receives $|AG|_2$ units of the second commodity for $|AG|_1$ of the first (G being the midpoint of AF). Clearly such a trade is feasible, and the figure shows that it is preferred to B by all members of the coalition. This means that B is dominated through this coalition, so is not in the core.

Just as we may replicate once to obtain the economy $(\Pi, R)^2$ we may do so again to obtain $(\Pi, R)^3$, and so on; we may thus define a sequence of economies $(\Pi, R)^t$, for $t = 1, 2, \ldots$. Associated with this sequence of economies we have a sequence of cores, that is sets of states of the form

$$(x^{11}, \ldots x^{1t}, \ldots x^{m1}, \ldots x^{mt}).$$

If we want to compare the cores of different replications we must reduce them to the same dimensionality. As might be expected from the above example, we are able to do this by noting that any co-operative equilibrium assigns the same consumptions to all consumers of the same type, say x^i to type i, so we may represent the core of any replication, that is any $(\Pi, R)^t$, by an m-tuple $(x^1, \ldots x^m)$. The reasoning for this equal treatment in the core is the same as in the two-consumer example.

Proposition 4.2 Identical consumers have identical consumptions at a co-operative equilibrium of a replicated economy.

Proof We must show that if

$$X = (x^{11}, \ldots x^{1t}, \ldots x^{m1}, \ldots x^{mt})$$

is a co-operative equilibrium of $(\Pi, R)^t$ then, for each h, $x^{hs} = x^h$ for each s. If x^{k1} and x^{k2}, say, are distinct then they are not indifferent for type k, for otherwise $\frac{1}{2}(x^{k1} + x^{k2})$ would be preferred by both consumers $k1$ and $k2$, by convexity, and could also be attained by trading only with each other, so that X could not be a co-operative equilibrium. Now assume that $x^{k1} \pi x^{k2}$ and, for each h, let $x'(h)$ be the least preferred (according to $\bar{\pi}^h$) of the various x^{hs} with $x''(h)$ the average of these x^{hs} ($s = 1, \ldots t$). Then by convexity

$$x''(h) \; \bar{\pi}^h \; x'(h)$$

for each h, with strict preference for $h = k$; also

$$t\Sigma_h x''(h) = \Sigma_h \Sigma_s x^{hs} \leqq t\Sigma_h r^h$$

since X is feasible. It follows that a coalition of the least favoured consumers of each type would prefer and could achieve an average allocation, so would block X.

This proposition indicates the 'fairness' of co-operative equilibria. It is also useful for our analysis, for it allows us to compare the cores of different replications in an obvious way, and to conceive of an allocation as being in the cores of many replications. If an allocation is a co-operative equilibrium for all replications of an economy it is an asymptotic co-operative equilibrium for the economy; the asymptotic core of the economy is the set of such states. Thus an asymptotic co-operative equilibrium is the equilibrium which will obtain however large the economy, that is however little effect each individual's actions have.

Definition The allocation X is an asymptotic co-operative equilibrium of the economy (Π, R) if the mt-tuple

$$(x^1, \ldots x^1, \ldots x^m, \ldots x^m)$$

is a co-operative equilibrium for the replicated economy $(\Pi, R)^t$ for every t.

4.4 EDGEWORTH'S CONJECTURE

We may now demonstrate the basic result of this chapter, that when the economy becomes sufficiently large the co-operative equilibria which will emerge are precisely the competitive equilibria. This provides a rationale for studying competitive economies, and shows that the competitive equilibrium is particularly robust: all collusion and attempts to create monopoly power will not affect the competitive outcome.

Before demonstrating this result, it is worth noting that an asymptotic co-operative equilibrium does in fact exist. This is immediate from the existence of the same competitive equilibrium for each replicated economy, which is easy to show, and the fact that a competitive equilibrium is a co-operative equilibrium. We now show that, in the limit, a co-operative equilibrium is a competitive equilibrium. Just as the demonstration that a competitive equilibrium is a co-operative equilibrium (Proposition 4.1) was parallel to the demonstration that a competitive equilibrium is an optimum (Proposition 3.4), the proof of the proposition that an asymptotic co-operative equilibrium is a competitive equilibrium is quite similar to the proof that an optimum is a competitive equilibrium (Proposition 3.5); this also explains the positivity qualification.

Proposition 4.3 A positive asymptotic co-operative equilibrium is a competitive equilibrium.

Proof We must show that if $\bar{X}$ is an asymptotic co-operative equilibrium for (Π, R) with each $\bar{x}^h > 0$ then, for some p, $(p, \bar{X})$ is a competitive equilibrium. Let

$$S^h = \{z^h = x^h - r^h \mid x^h \pi \bar{x}^h\}$$

be the set of 'better trades' for h and define

$$S = \{z = \Sigma a_h z^h \mid z^h \in S^h \text{ for each } h, a \in Q_1\}$$

(Q_1 being the unit simplex). Now if there were some negative $z \in S$ there would be some corresponding x with each $x^h \pi \bar{x}^h$ and some $a \in Q_1$ such that

$$\Sigma a_h x^h < \Sigma a_h r^h.$$

Then (noting Problem 2, Chapter 1) we may approximate a by a/ae for some vector a of positive integers and have

$$\Sigma a_h x^h < \Sigma a_h r^h.$$

Now consider a coalition of ae consumers, consisting of a_h of each type h: its resources are $\Sigma a_h r^h$, so it could distribute x^h to each consumer of type h, and since $x^h \pi \bar{x}^h$ this would be socially preferred; the coalition would therefore have blocked the allocation $\bar{X}$. It follows that S contains no $z < 0$. Since convexity of preferences implies that S is also convex, Minkowski's theorem ensures that there is some $p \geq 0$ such that $pz \geq 0$ for every $z \in S$. Because each $S^h \subset S$, by setting $a_h = 1$, this means that

$$px^h \geq pr^h$$

for every $x^h \pi \bar{x}^h$; an argument exactly parallel to that used in Proposition 3.5 shows that this inequality also holds for every $x^h \tilde{\pi} \bar{x}^h$, including $\bar{x}^h$. It follows that

$$p\bar{x}^h \geq pr^h$$

for each h, and therefore, since $\bar{x} = r$, that

$$p\bar{x}^h = pr^h$$

and each budget constraint is satisfied. Finally, for any x^h satisfying the budget constraint,

$$p\lambda x^h < pr^h$$

when $0 < \lambda < 1$. Since $px^h \geq pr^h$ for every $x^h \tilde{\pi} \bar{x}^h$ this means that $\bar{x}^h \pi \lambda x^h$, and in the limit as $\lambda \to 1$, $\bar{x}^h \tilde{\pi} x^h$, which is to say that, for each h, $\bar{x}^h$ maximises preference subject to the budget constraint. It follows that $(p, \bar{X})$ is a competitive equilibrium.

In the case where all utility functions u^h are differentiable a simpler demonstration is available. If $\bar{X}$ is an asymptotic co-operative equilibrium then it is an optimum, and is therefore sustained by a price vector p. If it is not a competitive equilibrium then, for some type h, we must have

$$p\bar{x}^h < pr^h.$$

From this and the differentiability of u^h it is not difficult to show that $\bar{X}$ is blocked by a coalition consisting of t consumers of type h and $t-1$ of each of the other types, where t is a sufficiently large integer.

4.5 PRODUCTION

Production is introduced through the concept of personal production: instead of consumer h owning a share s^{hk} of the profit of producer k, who has production set Y^k, we consider the consumer as owning the production set

$$s^{hk}Y^k = \{s^{hk}y^k | y^k \in Y^k\},$$

that is being able to avail himself of any production in this set. Since this applies to all the producers in which the consumer owns shares, the consumer owns many such sets; we therefore consider him as owning the sum

$$A^h = \Sigma_k s^{hk} Y^k.$$

This concept allows us to proceed in the same way as in the exchange case: we simply replace the set of resources available to consumer h, which was $\{r^h\}$, with $\{r^h\} + A^h$. For this construction to be consistent we must check that

$$A^S = \Sigma_S A^h \subset \Sigma_M A^h = A$$

for any coalition $S \subset M$, and that these two sets are the same when $S = M$; this is quite straightforward. This means that, given any two disjoint coalitions S and T, any $y^S \in A^S$ and any $y^T \in A^T$, as well as their sum $y^S + y^T$, are feasible and can be produced independently from each other.

An economy is now an array (Π, R, S, Γ), but an allocation is still a consumption array and a coalition still a subset of the set of consumers. An allocation X dominates X' if there is a coalition S which socially prefers X to X' and can achieve X by themselves, either by trading or production, that is if

$$\Sigma_S x^h \leq \Sigma_S r^h + a^S$$

for some $a^S \in A^S$. The allocation X is a co-operative equilibrium if it is undominated, and it is feasible (in that

$$x \leq r + a$$

for some $a \in A$). Clearly this is a special case of an optimum, so a co-operative equilibrium is still an optimum. Also, Proposition 4.1 carries over immediately, so a competitive equilibrium remains a co-operative equilibrium. This Proposition is extended in exactly the same way as was the parallel Proposition 3.4.

We may replicate the production economy (Π, R, S, Γ) in exactly the same way as we replicated the exchange economy (Π, R). For every consumer with the characteristics $(\tilde{\pi}^h, r^h, s^h)$ we add a further $t-1$ identical consumers, and for every producer with the production set Y^k we add $t-1$ identical producers. Then Proposition 4.2, on the equality of consumptions for each individual of a given type, carries over trivially. This is because if we had an inequality of such consumptions we could still find a dominating allocation simply by rearrangement of consumptions, that is without disturbing productions. Thus we may again conceive of a co-operative equilibrium of the basic economy being one of a replicated economy, and define an asymptotic co-operative equilibrium as an allocation which is a co-operative equilibrium for all replications. We may then show that a positive asymptotic co-operative equilibrium is still a competitive equilibrium, or that the core of the production economy shrinks in the limit to the set of competitive equilibria. Again, Proposition 4.3 is extended in exactly the same way as was the parallel Proposition 3.5.

Notes
1 The framework of this chapter was suggested by F. Y. Edgeworth [*Mathematical Psychics*, London, 1881] but not formalised until much later. The approach here is that of G. Debreu and H. Scarf [A Limit Theorem on the Core of an Economy, *International Economic Review*, 1963], who also weaken some of the axioms. It is not easy to relax these as much as those required for the competitive equilibrium, though we may weaken monotonicity for consumers and convexity for producers, and incorporate production sets. This is done by W. Hildenbrand [*Core and Equilibria of a Large Economy*, Princeton, 1974].
2 An alternative and more powerful way to formalise the concept of an individual being small is to consider a continuum of agents, where the competitive and co-operative equilibria are immediately identical; this is shown by R. J. Aumann [Markets with a Continuum of Traders, *Econometrica*, 1964]. Yet a third method which embraces both the discrete and continuous approaches by using non-standard analysis is that of D. J. Brown and A. Robinson [Nonstandard Exchange Economies, *Econometrica*, 1975].

Problems
1 In the context of Figure 4.1 show that the core is the set of points represented by the heavy curve, and that a competitive equilibrium does exist.
2 Show that a competitive equilibrium of an economy is also a competitive equilibrium of all replications of the economy.
3 Show that the core of an economy is closed and bounded.
4 Show that the set of utilities associated with the core of an economy,

$\{(u^1(x^1), \ldots u^m(x^m)) \mid X$ is a co-operative equilibrium$\}$,

is weakly convex.
5 A set V is a solution set of the economy if no allocation in V dominates another in V and if all allocations not in V are

dominated by some allocation in V. Show that the core is a subset of any solution set.
6 Show that a solution set (see Problem 5) of a two-consumer economy is also a solution set of all replications of the economy.
7 Complete the demonstration of Proposition 4.3 in the simple case when all utility functions are differentiable.
8 If
$$A^h = \Sigma_k s^{hk} Y^k$$
show that
$$\Sigma_S A^h \subset \Sigma_M A^h$$
for all coalitions $S \subset M$, with equality when $S = M$.
9 Show that a competitive equilibrium is a co-operative equilibrium in a production economy.
10 Show that a positive asymptotic co-operative equilibrium is a competitive equilibrium in a production economy.

5 Dynamic Equilibrium

We now turn from the competitive or abstractly co-operative framework to the explicitly monopolistic, and consider the interaction of individuals who have more say about their environment. The consideration of monopoly is of course important in its own right, but this is not the main reason for considering this problem. The more basic reason is that there is a certain dilemma associated with the notion of competitive equilibrium as a price system at which the economy is at rest: if no one can affect prices the economy must be at rest at any price system. With monopoly, however, prices are influenced, so we are able to consider the stationary state aspect of equilibrium more properly, that is investigate the dynamic equilibrium. We commence with a discussion of the relevance of this, then show the existence of such an equilibrium and some of its properties. For simplicity of exposition we consider only the exchange economy.

5.1 CONCEPTS

In Chapter 3 we noted two main reasons for being concerned with the existence of equilibrium; the discussion there implicitly stressed the normative reason, the possibility of order. Here we are more concerned with the positive reason, that most meaningful predictions concern states at which the economy is at rest, or in balance. We therefore consider equilibrium as a state from which there is no movement.

Clearly such a formulation requires that we specify the laws of movement, or dynamics of the economy. This contrasts with the competitive analysis of Chapter 3 and the co-operative of Chapter 4, both of which were essentially static (though capable of being made dynamic). It follows that if we consider different dynamics, or laws of movement, for the same static economy (preferences and resources) we may define different equilibria. For some laws of movement this dynamic equilibrium may satisfy the static no excess demands condition, but for others it may not. A particular application of this is that it allows us to consider the Keynesian problem of chronic unemployment (or equilibrium excess demand), which is of course meaningless in the static model.

The essence of the discussion then becomes the specification of the laws of movement. As we have noted, no one can change prices in a competitive economy, so there can be no movement. This is why we must turn to monopoly, though this in itself suggests a deeper reason for considering monopoly. In a finite economy any individual's action must affect prices, so the notion of competition itself in a finite economy is, at least in one sense, inconsistent. With monopoly we do not face this problem: by definition, a monopolist influences prices, and thus brings about movement.

An immediate extension of this is that it allows us to consider the stability of the economy with no further specification: a stable state is one to which there is movement, while an equilibrium state is one from which there is no movement. Clearly a stable state is an equilibrium state, but not conversely. Equilibrium and stability thus become essentially interrelated; it is therefore quite natural to go from the equilibrium discussion of this chapter to the stability discussion of Chapter 6. Thus the subject matter of this chapter may be interpreted in three ways: as an examination of the concept of dynamic equilibrium, as the analysis of general equilibrium with monopoly, or as the specification of a natural stability process.

5.2 ABSTRACT FRAMEWORK

Before considering the economy in more detail it is helpful to formalise some of these concepts in a more abstract framework (the notation of which is distinct from that of the proceeding and subsequent concrete analysis).

There are m agents, indexed by $h = 1, \ldots m$, each of whom takes some action at each point of a sequence of times, labelled $t = 0, 1, \ldots$. The action taken by agent h at time t is $a_h(t)$, an element of some given action space A_h, so that a state of the economy is given by the array of these actions, that is by

$$a(t) = (a_1(t), \ldots a_m(t)),$$

an element of the product space $A = A_1 \times \ldots A_m$. The action an agent takes is the most preferred of those available to him. This is most preferred if it is maximal with respect to some given ordering $\tilde{\pi}_h$ on the set of states A. It is available if it is an element of his choice set, a subset of his action space A_h; of course, for the construction to be interesting the actions available to the agent will depend on those taken by other agents, or on the existing state of the economy, so his choice set, for time t, is $\psi_h(a(t-1))$, where ψ_h is some given rule associating some subset of A_h with each element of A. The agent's action rule is therefore to choose that $a_h(t)$ which is $\tilde{\pi}_h$-maximal on $\psi_h(a(t-1))$, and, providing such a unique maximum exists, may therefore be represented by a function φ_h from A to A_h.

This means that given an existing state $a(t-1)$ the independent optimising actions of the individual agents define a new state

$$a(t) = \varphi(a(t-1)) = (\varphi_1(a(t-1)), \ldots \varphi_m(a(t-1))),$$

which in turn generates a succeeding state

$$a(t+1) = \varphi(a(t)),$$

and so on. Thus φ may be interpreted as a generating function of the economy. A dynamic equilibrium may now be more formally defined as a state which generates itself, that is an a with the property that $a = \varphi(a)$. It is clear then that a dynamic equilibrium is simply a fixed point of the generating function, so in demonstrating the existence of such an equilibrium we need only look for a fixed point of this given mapping, rather than search for an appropriate mapping as in the competitive case.

We may note that a dynamic equilibrium may equivalently be defined as a state which each agent (weakly) prefers to that which would result from any unilateral move, that is an a with the property that, for each h,

$$(a_1, \ldots a_h, \ldots a_m) \, \tilde{\pi}_h \, (a_1, \ldots a'_h, \ldots a_m)$$

for every $a'_h \in \psi_h(a)$. (Thus the dynamic equilibrium is equivalent to the Nash equilibrium of game theory, just as the co-operative equilibria correspond to the core.)

Any given state $a(0)$ in effect generates a sequence of states

$$a(1) = \varphi(a(0)), \ a(2) = \varphi(a(1)) = \varphi^2(a(0)), \ldots$$

It is clear then that a state a is stable if this sequence tends to it, that is if $\varphi^t(a(0)) \to a$ as $t \to \infty$ for every $a(0) \in A$. This makes clear the relation between equilibrium and stability and that this is a truly dynamic equilibrium.

This abstract framework may be illustrated by a simple example. There are two agents ($h = 1, 2$), and each action space has two elements, say

$$A_h = (\alpha_h, \beta_h).$$

Agents have identical preferences which are represented by the common utility function u given by

$$u(\alpha_1, \alpha_2) = u(\beta_1, \beta_2) = 0$$
$$u(\alpha_1, \beta_2) = 1, \ u(\beta_1, \alpha_2) = 2,$$

and their choice sets are trivially their action spaces, that is $\psi_h \equiv A_h$. It is clear that the state (α_1, β_2) is an equilibrium, for

$$u(\alpha_1, \beta_2) > u(\alpha_1, \alpha_2),$$
$$u(\alpha_1, \beta_2) > u(\beta_1, \beta_2)$$

so no agent desires to change his action unilaterally and the state is maintained. However, it is equally clear that the state (β_1, α_2) is also an equilibrium, and indeed one which is preferred by both agents to the former equilibrium. Further, it is easy to see that neither of the other possible states are equilibria, and also that neither of these generate sequences with limits, which means that neither equilibrium is stable. Thus, in general, even should an equilibrium exist it need not be unique, optimal, or stable.

Finally, it is worth examining a special form of this framework which is particularly relevant where it is useful to distinguish between prices and quantities. Here a state α is partitioned into two components (α^1, α^2). Then given the existing state

$$(\alpha^1(t-1), \alpha^2(t-1))$$

each agent h first chooses α_h^1 to be $\tilde{\pi}_h^1$-maximal on

$$\psi_h^1(\alpha^1(t-1), \alpha^2(t-1))$$

thus together generating $\alpha^1(t)$, then chooses α_h^2 to be $\tilde{\pi}_h^2$-maximal on

$$\psi_h^2(\alpha^1(t), \alpha^2(t-1))$$

thus together generating $\alpha^2(t)$, and therefore $\alpha(t)$ (where the components $\tilde{\pi}_h^k$ and ψ_h^k for $k = 1, 2$, are defined in an obvious way). Of course in general $\alpha^2(t)$ will depend on $\alpha^1(t)$ and $\alpha^2(t-1)$, but if in fact $\alpha^2(t)$ can be written as a function of $\alpha^1(t)$ alone, then an equilibrium of the subsystem $\alpha^1(t)$ will imply that of the whole system $\alpha(t)$: specifically,

$$\alpha^1(t) = \alpha^1(t-1)$$

will imply
$$\alpha^2(t) = \varphi'(\alpha^1(t)) = \varphi'(\alpha^1(t-1)) = \alpha^2(t-1)$$

so that
$$\alpha(t) = \alpha(t-1).$$

Further, if the function φ' is continuous, then $\alpha^1(t) \to \alpha^1$ will imply $\alpha(t) \to \alpha$, so that the stability of the subsystem $\alpha^1(t)$ will determine that of the whole system $\alpha(t)$.

The relevance of this is seen by interpreting α^1 as prices and α^2 as quantities. Then given some existing state, each agent first chooses various prices, in a profit-maximising manner, thus generating a new price system. Given this new price system, and possibly the existing quantities, he then chooses new quantities, in a preference-maximising manner, thus generating a new quantity system, and therefore a new state. In fact in some interesting cases the quantity decision will depend only on the new prices, so that the behaviour of the price subsystem will determine the behaviour of the whole economy.

5.3 MONOPOLY

The necessary monopolistic element is introduced by distinguishing commodities on the basis of ownership as well as by their other characteristics. This means that there is only one seller of a commodity, so we move from the one polar case of pure competition to the other of pure monopoly. The seller quotes prices for his commodities, specifically those prices which he perceives will maximise his revenue. This requires that he perceive some relationship between the prices he quotes and the resultant demands. The seller naturally knows the 'position' of these perceived demand curves, since he knows the prices he quoted (and all other prices) and the resulting demands in the existing state of the economy. The subjective part concerns the 'slopes': as an approximation, it is assumed that the seller perceives demand to decrease linearly in own price and to be independent of other prices. It is easy to see that this implies that he chooses the price of each commodity he sells to maximise the perceived revenue from that commodity. Thus without loss of generality we may consider each agent as owning only one commodity; since no two agents own the same commodity we may then identify commodities with agents.

Given an existing state each agent chooses a price in this manner, thus determining his perceived revenue, or wealth. Then given this resulting price system and associated wealths each consumer chooses a consumption to be preference-maximal subject to its cost not exceeding his wealth. This generates a new allocation, and thus a new state.

However, the trades implied by this process are only notional, so that the original endowments, and thus economy, remain. Since we are concerned with states at which there is no movement anyway this artificial device is acceptable here. For the time being we ignore the question of whether these prices are abstract or numeraire prices, but later show that the entire discussion may be interpreted in terms of numeraire prices. This is consistent with perceived demand curves being homogeneous.

Consumers and commodities are now identified by the single index $i = 1, \ldots n$. Consumer i chooses a price p_i for his commodity and a consumption x^i; a state of the economy is therefore given by (p, X). Then given the existing state

$$(p(t-1), X(t-1))$$

consumer i chooses $p_i(t)$ to maximise his perceived revenue $p_i(t)\hat{x}_i(t)$, where $\hat{x}_i(t)$ is his perceived demand, given by

$$\hat{x}_i(t) = x_i(t-1) - a_i(p_i(t) - p_i(t-1));$$

here

$$a_i = -d\hat{x}_i/dp_i > 0$$

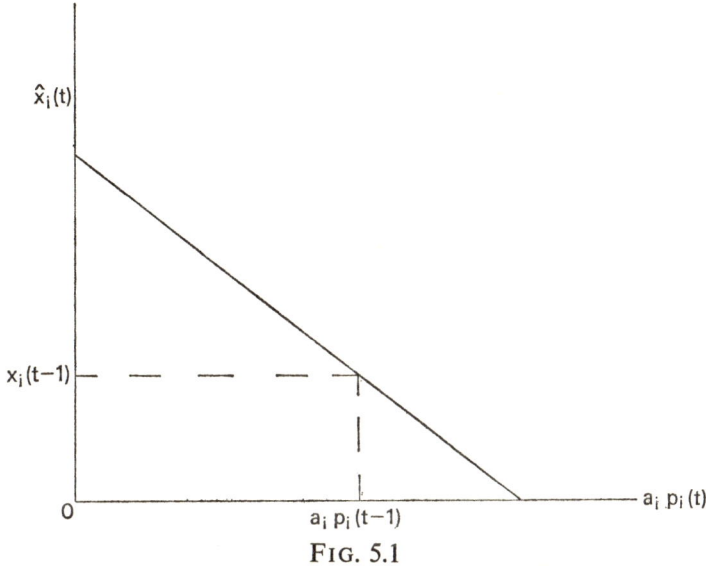

Fig. 5.1

is the given (downward) slope of his perceived demand curve for his commodity. This is illustrated in Figure 5.1. Together this generates the new price system $p(t)$. Consumer i then chooses $x^i(t)$ to be $\hat{\pi}^i$-maximal on his available consumption set.

Consumer i's choice of p_i is constrained by the requirement that perceived demand not exceed his resources, that is by $\hat{x}_i(t) \leq r_i$. The non-negativity of $\hat{x}_i$ does not require mention, as it is clear that any effectively chosen $\hat{x}_i$ will be positive, as will any chosen p_i. His choice of x^i is constrained by the requirement that its cost not exceed his perceived revenue or wealth, that is by

$$p(t) x^i(t) = p_i(t)\hat{x}_i(t)$$

(because of monotonicity there is no increase in generality in replacing this equality with a weak inequality).

It is straightforward to compute the solution to the price-choice problem as

$$p_i(t) = \max \{\tfrac{1}{2}(x_i(t-1)/a_i + p_i(t-1)), (x_i(t-1) - r_i)/a_i + p_i(t-1)\};$$

this is illustrated in Figure 5.2 where $p_i(t)$ is the price chosen, given the perceived demand curve D and $p'_i(t)$ that given D'. Then by

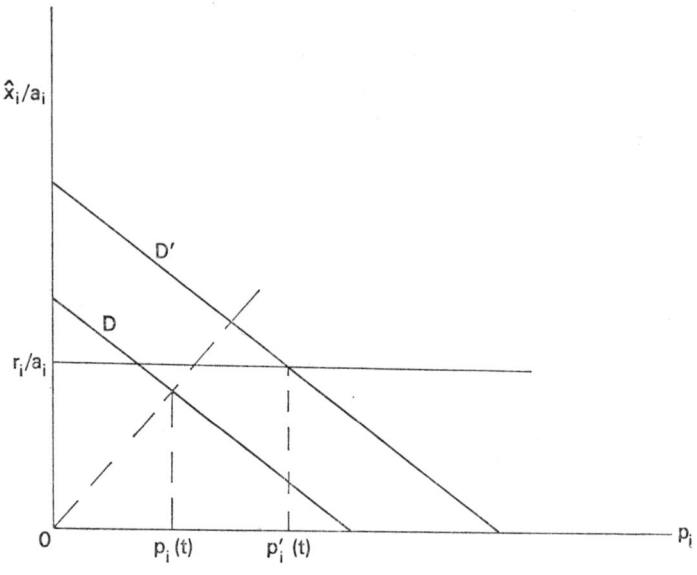

FIG. 5.2

substitution perceived demand is

$$\hat{x}_i(t) = \min \{a_i p_i(t), r_i\},$$

and therefore perceived wealth is

$$p_i(t) \hat{x}_i(t) = \min \{a_i p_i(t)^2, p_i(t) r_i\}.$$

Thus wealth at time t depends only on prices at time t, and as $x^i(t)$ is chosen subject only to $p(t)x^i(t)$ not exceeding wealth at time t, it follows that consumption at time t may be written as a function of prices at time t alone.

Definition The monopoly demand function (for consumer i) $x^i(p)$ is defined by $x^i(p)$ is $\tilde{\pi}^i$-maximal on

$$\{x^i | px^i = \min \{a_i p_i^2, p_i r_i\}\}.$$

DYNAMIC EQUILIBRIUM

It is straightforward to show, following the argument of Chapter 2, that this is well-defined, at least for positive prices, which is sufficient. Not surprisingly, it is also continuous.

Proposition 5.1 An individual monopoly demand function is continuous.

Proof It was shown in Proposition 2.2 that the function $x(p, a(p))$ defined by $x(p, a(p))$ is $\tilde{\pi}$-maximal on

$$\{x \mid px = a(p)\}$$

is continuous if $a(p)$ is positive and continuous. But $a(p)$ is simply

$$\min \{a_i p_i^2, p_i r_i\}$$

which is clearly positive and continuous for $p > 0$, which is sufficient.

In the general framework of the preceding section the actions a_i^1 and a_i^2 are p_i and x^i; the preferences $\tilde{\pi}_i^1$ and $\tilde{\pi}_i^2$ are defined by

$$a_i^1 \; \tilde{\pi}_i^1 \; \bar{a}_i^1 \text{ if } p_i \; \hat{x}_i(p_i) \geqq \bar{p}_i \; \hat{x}_i(\bar{p}_i),$$

$$a_i^2 \; \tilde{\pi}_i^2 \; \bar{a}_i^2 \text{ if } x^i \; \tilde{\pi}^i \; \bar{x}^i;$$

and the choice sets ψ_i^1 and ψ_i^2 are given by

$$\psi_i^1(a) = \{p_i \geqq 0 \mid x_i(p_i) \leqq r_i\},$$

$$\psi_i^2(a) = \{x^i \mid px^i = \min \{a_i p_i^2, p_i r_i\}\}.$$

Since we have shown that, for each i, $x^i(t)$ is a continuous function of $p_i(t)$ alone (for $p(t) > 0$, and that in fact $p(t) > 0$ for all t) it is clear that $a^2(t)$ is a continuous function of $a^1(t)$ alone. It follows that we need only consider the behaviour of the subsystem $a^1(t)$, that is the price system $p(t)$.

5.4 EXISTENCE

To examine the existence of a dynamic equilibrium we must specify the action rules φ_i of the abstract framework, and thus the generating function, more explicitly. However, since the quantity actions $a^2(t)$ are simply continuous functions of the price actions $a^1(t)$, we need only consider the price generating function. This is immediately given from the individual price choices discussed in the preceding section, together with the monopoly demand functions. An equilibrium is then a fixed point of this generating function.

An economy is now defined not only by preferences and resources, but also by the (slopes of the) perceived demand curves, that is the array $a = (a_1, \ldots a_n)$; thus an economy is a triple (Π, R, a). Further, since consumers are now identified with the commodities they own, the $n \times n$ matrix $R = [r_i^h]$ is diagonal.

Definition The pair (p, X) is a dynamic equilibrium of the economy (Π, R, a) if $p = f(p)$, where f is the generating function of the economy defined by, for each i,

$$f_i(p) = \max \{\tfrac{1}{2}(x_i(p)/a_i + p_i), (x_i(p) - r_i)/a_i + p_i\}.$$

An equivalent interpretation of an equilibrium and of the generating function is obtained from the expression for perceived demand derived in the preceding section. Using this it is straightforward to obtain

$$f(p) - p = B(p)(x - \hat{x})$$

where $B(p)$ is a diagonal matrix with elements

$$b_{ii} = 1/2a_i \text{ if } p_i < r_i/a_i,$$
$$b_{ii} = 1/a_i \text{ if } p_i \geq r_i/a_i.$$

From this it is immediate that p is an equilibrium if $x = \hat{x}$, that is if all expectations are fulfilled. Further, if we interpret x as 'supply', then prices are adjusted in proportion to excess demands, at least locally.

It is important to note that these excess demands satisfy Walras' law, that is that

$$px \equiv p\hat{x}.$$

However, this does not imply that

$$pf(p) \equiv pp,$$

but it does imply a 'weak Walras' law'.

Proposition 5.2 If all markets but one are stationary then all markets are stationary.

Proof We must show that $f_i(p) = p_i$ for all $i < n$ implies $f_n(p) = p_n$. Adding the individual budget constraints

$$px^i = p_i \hat{x}_i$$

gives

$$p(x - \hat{x}) = 0$$

so that if

$$b_{ii} p_i (x_i - \hat{x}_i) = 0$$

for each $i < n$ then

$$b_{nn} p_n (x_n - \hat{x}_n) = 0$$

where the b_{ii} are any non-zero weights. The result then follows from noting that $f(p) - p$ may be written as $B(p)(x - \hat{x})$, where B is a positive diagonal matrix.

The importance of this is that it allows us to consider numeraire prices, since there is no danger that the numeraire commodity, whose price must be fixed, will be out of equilibrium when other prices are in equilibrium.

Since the artificial mapping constructed to show the existence of a competitive equilibrium in Chapter 3, and which had a fixed point, is quite similar to this, it is not surprising that this mapping has a fixed point, so that a dynamic equilibrium exists. To see this we first consider the modified generating function which always reduces $f(p)$ to the same scale as p, and show that this has a fixed point. This means that there is some p which generates a positive multiple of itself; the weak Walras' law then shows that this multiple must be unity. Note that, unlike the competitive case, we cannot require positive endowments, since $r_j^i = 0$ whenever $i \neq j$.

Proposition 5.3 An economy has a dynamic equilibrium for any scale of prices.

Proof We must show that for every $\mu > 0$ there exists some $p \geq 0$ such that $f(p) = p$ and $pe = \mu$. Each $x^i(p)$ is continuous from Proposition 5.1, so that $x(p)$ is continuous. It follows that $f(p)$ is continuous, as therefore is $f'(p)$, defined on the simplex Q_μ by

$$f'(p) = \mu f(p)/f(p)e.$$

Clearly f' maps from Q_μ to itself, and therefore has a fixed point, by Brouwer's theorem. This means there is some $p \in Q_\mu$ such that

$$f(p) = \lambda p$$

where

$$\lambda = f(p)\,e/\mu > 0.$$

Then, in the notation of Proposition 5.2,

$$f(p) - p = (\lambda - 1)p = B(x - \hat{x})$$

so that by use of this proposition,

$$(\lambda - 1)pB^{-1}p = p(x - \hat{x}) = 0;$$

then since $pB^{-1}p > 0$ it follows that $\lambda = 1$, so that $f(p) = p$.

We may now interpret p as a numeraire price. If commodity n is the numeraire the generating function f is modified to f' where $f'_i = f_i$ for each $i < n$ and $f'_n \equiv 1$. Proposition 5.2 provides a formal justification for this; from a point of view of interpretation some agent (or institution) must be understood as undertaking this quasi-monetary role for its commodity (gold). The demonstration of the existence of a numeraire equilibrium is not quite as straightforward as in the competitive case, since demands are clearly not homogeneous, and the fact that p is an equilibrium price at the scale of prices μ does not imply that λp is at the scale $\lambda\mu$.

Proposition 5.4 An economy has a numeraire dynamic equilibrium.

Proof We must show that, for some j, there exists some p such that $f(p) = p$ and $p_j = 1$. We first show that the equilibrium $p(\mu)$ is continuous in the scale μ. Let $\mu^t \to \mu$ and

then by definition
$$p^t = p(\mu^t) \to p;$$
$$p^t = \mu^t f(p^t)/f(p^t)e,$$

so taking limits and using the continuity of f we have

$$p = \mu f(p)/f(p)e$$

so that $p = p(\mu)$. Now if $\mu < 1$ then $p_i < 1$ for each i, while if $\mu > n$ then $p_j > 1$ for some j; then by continuity there is some intermediary μ such that $p_j = 1$ for the appropriate j. This defines the numeraire equilibrium.

This is the basic result on the dynamic equilibrium; in the light of this, and the weak Walras' law, all prices are to be interpreted throughout as numeraire prices.

5.5 PROPERTIES

The most important general property of the dynamic equilibrium is that it may be a monopolistic equilibrium in the sense that it may involve some of the potential supply of various commodities being held back from the market in order to raise their sellers' wealths. Equilibrium is characterised by the fulfilment of all expectations, that is by $x = \hat{x}$, while $\hat{x}_i$ is given from the price-choice problems as min $\{a_i p_i, r_i\}$. It follows that if $p_i < r_i/a_i$ at equilibrium we will have $x_i < r_i$, that is some of commodity i is held back from the market, and commodity i is 'monopolistic'. On the other hand if $p_i \geq r_i/a_i$ at equilibrium, then we will have $x_i = r_i$, so commodity i is 'competitive', and also x^i will be $\bar{\pi}^i$-maximal on

$$\{x^i | px^i = pr^i\},$$
since
$$p_i r_i = pr^i.$$

DYNAMIC EQUILIBRIUM

If this holds for all i then clearly the dynamic equilibrium is a competitive equilibrium, which means that the dynamic equilibrium will be an optimum if all commodities are competitive. Thus the dynamic equilibrium is an extension of the concept of competitive equilibrium.

This may be illustrated by the two-commodity (and therefore two-consumer) Cobb–Douglas economy defined by

$$u^h(x^h) = x_1^h x_2^h \ (h = 1, 2),$$
$$R = ((1, 0), (0, 2)),$$

with perceived slopes given by $a = e$ (commodity two is the numeraire). We may compute the competitive equilibrium for the scale of prices μ to be $(\tfrac{1}{3}\mu, \tfrac{2}{3}\mu)$, so the numeraire competitive equilibrium is $(\tfrac{1}{2}, 1)$ (see Problem 1, Chapter 3). However, the dynamic equilibrium is not proportional to the scale of prices. If $\mu \geq 6$ then each commodity is competitive, so the equilibrium is again $(\tfrac{1}{3}\mu, \tfrac{2}{3}\mu)$. If $\mu \leq 2$ then each commodity is monopolistic, and we may compute the dynamic equilibrium to be $\tfrac{1}{2}\mu e$. If however $2 < \mu < 6$ the first commodity is monopolistic and the second competitive, and the dynamic equilibrium is no longer linear in μ; it may be computed as (λ, λ^2) where

$$\lambda = \tfrac{1}{2}(4\mu + 1)^{1/2} - \tfrac{1}{2}.$$

The numeraire dynamic equilibrium is therefore e. This is illustrated in Figure 5.3, where P is the expansion path of equilibrium prices.

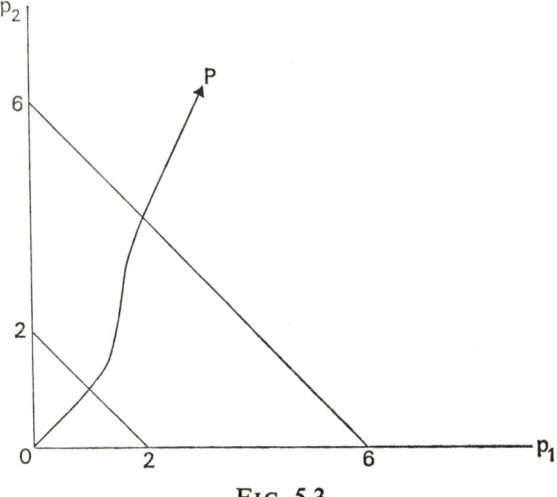

FIG. 5.3

This example shows that the dynamic equilibrium need not be optimal for at the numeraire equilibrium one half of the available amount of the first commodity is wasted, so each consumer could be made better off simply by distributing this in any way.

Since the dynamic equilibrium is identical with the competitive equilibrium when all commodities are competitive it is clear that, in this range, equilibrium is linear in the scale of prices. The example shows that this is not the case if one, but not all, commodity is monopolistic, but suggests that it may be the case if all commodities are monopolistic. However, this is not generally true, though one may show it to apply wherever all preferences may be represented by utility functions u^i with the property

$$u^i(\lambda x^i) = h^i(\lambda) u^i(x)$$

for some function h^i, that is when preferences are homothetic.

The dynamic equilibrium is an extension of the competitive equilibrium in that it allows all commodities to be monopolistic, or more importantly, some to be monopolistic and some competitive. It is also an extension in the sense that it is more likely to exist: every 'economy' (perhaps where the preference axioms are not satisfied) which has a competitive equilibrium has a dynamic equilibrium, but not conversely, though of course this only has meaning for economies which can be compared in both forms, that is where R is diagonal. The first part of this proposition follows from the fact that for some scale of prices the competitive and dynamic equilibria coincide, and the latter by counterexample.

Proposition 5.5 If an 'economy' has a competitive equilibrium then it has a dynamic equilibrium, but not conversely.

Proof Let $p > 0$ be a competitive equilibrium of the economy (Π, R, a) (essentially (Π, R)) and define

$$\alpha = \max_i r_i/a_i p_i.$$

Then

$$\alpha p_i \geq r_i/a_i$$

for each i, so all commodities are competitive at αp, and therefore, as αp is a competitive equilibrium, it is equivalently a dynamic equilibrium. Now consider the economy (Π, R, a) where (Π, R) is given in Problem 2 of Chapter 3 and $a = (1, \frac{1}{3})$, for example. From this problem, this economy has no competitive equilibrium; however, one may compute that it does have a numeraire dynamic equilibrium, specifically $(\lambda, 1)$ where $\lambda \approx 0.9$ (for the exact value see Problem 8).

Notes

1 The framework of this chapter was suggested by G. Debreu [A Social Equilibrium Existence Theorem, *Proceedings of the National Academy of Sciences of the USA*, 1952]; the approach taken here follows that of M. Allingham [*Equlibrium and Disequilibrium*, Cambridge (Mass.), 1973] where a more general treatment may be found. This requires only weak convexity, and more importantly, allows price and quantity choices to be simultaneous.
2 The incorporation of production is not in general particularly straightforward, as one cannot then use the separability of price and quantity decisions; see M. G. Allingham [Equilibrium and Stability, *Econometrica*, 1974].

Problems

1 In the abstract framework developed in this chapter show that every stable state is an equilibrium.
2 In the abstract framework developed in this chapter assume that $a^2 = \varphi'(a^1)$ and show that $a^1(t) \to a^1$ need not imply $a(t) \to a$ in general, but will if φ' is continuous.
3 Show that if p maximises $p\,\hat{x}$ then p_i maximises $p_i\,\hat{x}_i$ for each i.
4 Show that if p_i maximises $p_i\,\hat{x}_i$ then $p_i > 0$ and $\hat{x}_i > 0$.
5 Show that p may be a dynamic equilibrium without λp being for any positive $\lambda \neq 1$.
6 Show that the dynamic equilibria for every scale of prices of the Cobb–Douglas example discussed in this chapter are as stated.
7 Show that if all preferences are homothetic and p is a dynamic equilibrium at which all commodities are monopolistic then p is a dynamic equilibrium for every positive $\lambda < 1$.
8 Show that the numeraire dynamic equilibrium of the counter-example in Proposition 5.5 is $(\lambda, 1)$ where λ is the root of

$$3\lambda^3 + 3\lambda^2 - 4\lambda - 1 = 0$$

$(0 < \lambda < 1)$.

6 Stability

The discussion so far has concerned the existence of an equilibrium, in the appropriate sense, and some of its properties, but has ignored the question of whether such an equilibrium may be attained. The difference between existence and attainability, or stability, may be seen by analogy: an egg standing on its head may be in equilibrium, but will seldom arrive there. Whether it does arrive there depends on how it is moved, thus the discussion of stability requires a dynamic structure. We concentrate on the stability of the competitive equilibrium; since this has no implicit dynamic structure we introduce an external one, the tatonnement. This is then related to the stability of the dynamic equilibrium, which has its own implicit dynamic structure. Throughout we use the excess demand representation of the economy, and interpret all prices as numeraire prices.

6.1 TATONNEMENT

The basic question we consider is, given some arbitrary initial state, whether the economy will eventually move to an equilibrium; or equivalently, if the economy is disturbed from equilibrium by some temporary external shock, whether it will eventually return to equilibrium. Again this is relevant at both the normative and positive levels. At the former, it illustrates the relevance of such properties as the optimality of equilibrium: if equilibrium were not stable this would be of less interest. At the latter, it reinforces any comparative static predictions: a prediction of a new equilibrium which will result from some external shock is of less interest if this new equilibrium will not be attained. (It is also possible that the assumption of stability may imply some comparative static properties; this is considered in Chapter 7).

The essence of stability is the dynamic structure, since this, together with the excess demand function, forms a generating function for the economy. Then given some initial state (or price) a sequence of further states (or prices) is generated; in a loose sense the economy is stable if this tends to an equilibrium. The dynamic structure we examine is the Walrasian tatonnement, which simply changes prices in proportion to excess demands: increasing price when demand is too great and lowering price when demand is too low. Thus given a price p (and a corresponding excess demand $z(p)$) the Walrasian tatonnement in its simplest form changes prices by $A\, z(p)$, where A is a positive diagonal matrix of 'adjustment speeds' (though in fact we may choose units so that each of these is unity). However, since we interpret prices as numeraire prices (with numeraire n) this only applies to the non-numeraire commodities. A further modification, for simplicity, is to replace this implied difference equation by the corresponding differential equation. The process we consider then becomes

$$\dot{p}_i = z_i(p) \ (i < n),$$

$$p_n \equiv 1$$

(where $\dot{p} = dp/dt$).

We should check that the path $p(t)$ generated by this process is well-defined, specifically that prices remain positive and bounded along it (we take the existence of a unique continuous path as accepted). It is reasonable to take the initial price $p(0)$ as positive, since it could not possibly be an equilibrium otherwise. Then, since each $z_i(p)$ is continuous and $z_i(p) = \infty$ when $p_i = 0$, there is, for any given prices p_j ($j \neq i$), some $\delta > 0$ such that if $p_i < \delta$ then

$$z_i = \dot{p}_i > 0,$$

so that p_i is increasing. Since $p(t)$ is continuous in t this means that p_i could not fall below δ, so that $p(t) > 0$ for all t. The boundedness of $p(t)$ follows from Walras' law, since

$$d(pp)/dt = 2p\dot{p} = 2pz(p) = 0,$$

whence

$$p(t)\,p(t) = p(0)\,p(0)$$

for all t.

Care must be taken with the interpretation of the tatonnement from two aspects. Firstly, unlike the generating function associated with the dynamic equilibrium, this process, though quite plausible, is determined arbitrarily from outside the economy rather than by the agents themselves. This aspect may be given substance by considering the tatonnement to be operated by some external auctioneer. Secondly, in common with the dynamic equilibrium generating function, trade at the various temporary disequilibrium prices must be prohibited, for otherwise the distribution of resources R, and thus the economy (Π, R, S, Γ) would be changing; thus 'demands' must be interpreted as 'intended demands'. This aspect may be given substance by considering all commodities to be

6.2 LYAPOUNOV METHOD

It is clear that if $p(t)$ tends to some limit $\bar{p}$ then $\dot{p}$ tends to zero, so that $z(\bar{p}) = 0$ and $\bar{p}$ is an equilibrium. However, if $\bar{p}$ and $\bar{\bar{p}}$ are both equilibria then any path originating from $\bar{p}$ will remain at $\bar{p}$, and likewise for $\bar{\bar{p}}$, so that all paths cannot tend to $\bar{p}$ or all to $\bar{\bar{p}}$. This means that if we are to interpret stability as all paths having a limit which is independent of their initial position, and which is an equilibrium, then we must confine our attention to economies with unique equilibria.

Definition The unique equilibrium $\bar{p}$ of an economy z is stable if the paths generated from all initial prices by the system

$$\dot{p}_i = z_i(p) \ (i < n),$$

$$p_n \equiv 1$$

converge to $\bar{p}$.

It will generally be impracticable to demonstrate stability by solving the differential equation system to obtain an explicit form of the solution path. Instead, we may show stability from the existence of a decreasing Lyapounov function; a Lyapounov function is a non-negative continuous function of prices which is zero at and only at the equilibrium price and which has a continuous time derivative. If $V(p(t))$ is such a decreasing function then it tends to some limit, say $\bar{V}$. Now if $\bar{V} > 0$ then for sufficiently large t, say $t > T$, we will have

$$2\bar{V} \geqq V(p(t)) \geqq \bar{V}.$$

Since $\dot{V}$ is continuous it has a maximum, say α, on the closed (by the continuity of V) and bounded set

$$\{p \,|\, 2\bar{V} \geqq V(p) \geqq \bar{V}\},$$

and as this set cannot contain the equilibrium $\bar{p}$ this maximum must be negative, so that

$$\dot{V}(p(t)) \leqq \alpha < 0$$

for all $t > T$. But together with the continuity of V, this implies that

$$V(p(t)) \leqq V(p(T)) + \alpha(t - T) \to -\infty$$

which contradicts the non-negativity of V. It follows that

$$V(p(t)) \to \bar{V} = 0,$$

so that as V is continuous and $V(p) = 0$ if and only if $p = \bar{p}$ we have $p(t) \to \bar{p}$, and the equilibrium $\bar{p}$ is stable.

The definition of (global) stability requires convergence from all possible initial positions. While this is to be desired the weaker property of local stability may still be of interest: this only requires convergence from initial positions sufficiently close to the equilibrium. This would be relevant if equilibrium were not unique, for any separated equilibrium, while clearly not globally stable, may be locally stable. However, if the set of equilibria were convex, for example, then no interior equilibrium could be stable, so now we must confine our attention to economies whose equilibria are separated, or locally unique. Local stability would also be of practical relevance if it were believed that any external shocks moving the economy from its equilibrium were in some sense small. Clearly a stable equilibrium is locally stable, but not conversely.

To take advantage of the weaker conditions required for local stability we must assume that the excess demand function z is differentiable at the equilibrium p, when by the definition of a derivative we may approximate the excess demand function in the neighbourhood of equilibrium. This approximates z by

$$z(\bar{p}) + Z(p - \bar{p}) = Z(p - \bar{p})$$

(as $z(\bar{p}) = 0$), where Z is the approximating linear map, or derivative, of z, that is the Jacobian matrix

$$[z_{ij}] = [\partial z_i/\partial p_j] \ (i, j = 1, \ldots n)$$

evaluated at $\bar{p}$. Since p_n is fixed, and because Walras' law implies that $z_n = 0$ if each $z_i = 0$ $(i < n)$, we need only consider the stability of the non-numeraire part of the economy, that is the system

$$\dot{p} = Z(p - \bar{p})$$

where Z is the non-numeraire matrix $[z_{ij}]$ $(i, j < n)$ (and although we do not change the symbols it is understood that $p = (p_1, \ldots p_{n-1})$).

We may solve this linear system explicitly to obtain

$$p(t) = \bar{p} + e^{tZ}p(0),$$

since this clearly gives

$$\dot{p} = Ze^{tZ}p(0) = Z(p - \bar{p})$$

as required; this means that $p(t) \to \bar{p}$ if and only if $e^{tZ} \to 0$ (assuming that $p(0) \neq 0$). In other words the economy will be locally stable if and only if Z is a stable matrix, that is if all its characteristic roots have negative real parts.

6.3 GLOBAL STABILITY

Before considering the general case it is helpful to examine a two-commodity economy. As in Chapter 3, Walras' law and homogeneity mean that this may be represented by a single real function. A stable equilibrium is illustrated in Figure 6.1: the arrows representing the

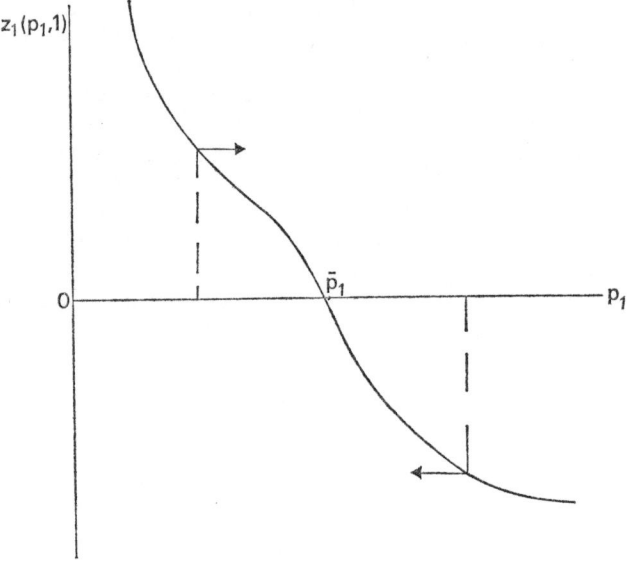

FIG. 6.1

direction of movement show that price is always increasing if it is below the equilibrium ($\bar{p}_1$) and decreasing if it is above, so that it must eventually come to equilibrium. Since excess demand must be positive at low prices and negative at high it is clear that, in this two-commodity economy, equilibrium must be stable if it is unique. Thus to illustrate an economy which is not stable we must drop uniqueness, as in Figure 6.2, where, though of course no equilibrium is stable, two equilibria ($\bar{p}_1$ and $\bar{p}_1''$) are locally stable and one ($\bar{p}_1'$) is not.

This suggests that it may be worth examining the uniqueness, or at least convexity, conditions of Chapter 3 to see if they also ensure stability. It was shown there that if an economy displays revealed preference then its set of equilibria is convex. If in fact this equilibrium is unique then it is straightforward to show that it is stable.

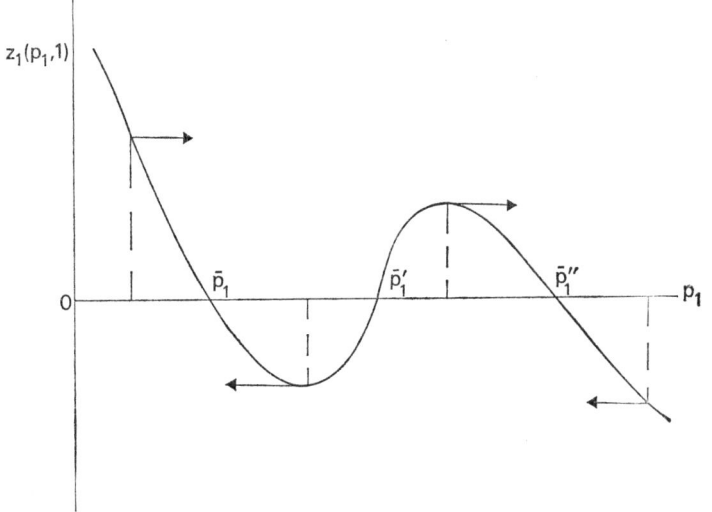

Fig. 6.2

Proposition 6.1 A unique equilibrium of a revealed preference economy is stable.

Proof Let $\bar{p}$ be the equilibrium price and define the Lyapounov function
$$V(p) = (p - \bar{p})(p - \bar{p}).$$
Then using Walras' law we have
$$\dot{V}(p) = 2(p - \bar{p})\dot{p} = 2(p - \bar{p})z(p) = -2\bar{p}z(p).$$
By revealed preference $\bar{p}z(p) > 0$ for all $p \neq \bar{p}$, so that $\dot{V} < 0$ and V is decreasing.

An application of this result is to the case where there is no trade at equilibrium (in an exchange economy). This would obtain if, in the light of Proposition 3.5, resources had been distributed to achieve an optimum before trade, or if all consumers were identical.

Proposition 6.2 A unique equilibrium at which there is no trade in an (exchange) economy is stable.

Proof If $\bar{p}$ is the equilibrium then $x^h(\bar{p}) = r^h$ for each h, so
$$px^h(\bar{p}) = pr^h$$
for all p. Since
$$px^h(p) = pr^h$$

for any p, we have

$$px^h(\bar{p}) \leqq px^h(p)$$

(in fact equality holds) so that, by individual revealed preference,

$$\bar{p}x^h(\bar{p}) < \bar{p}x^h(p)$$

provided that $p \neq \bar{p}$. Adding these inequalities, subtracting pr, and using Walras' law gives $0 < \bar{p}z(p)$, so that the economy displays revealed preference. Stability then follows from Proposition 6.1.

Since substitutability is stronger than revealed preference in ensuring uniqueness, it is worth considering whether the same is true for stability. We will in fact show directly that a substitutive economy is stable, but we first sketch this via our existing revealed preference result for the case where the excess demand function is differentiable.

Let $\bar{p}$ be the equilibrium of a substitutive economy and consider the value of $\bar{p}z(p)$. Since excess demands are bounded below, this clearly has a minimum for prices in the unit simplex, and indeed for all numeraire prices. Since excess demands are infinite at zero prices, and continuous, this minimum must be achieved where no price is at the (zero) boundary, and so be characterised by

$$\partial \bar{p}z(p)/\partial p_i = \Sigma_j \bar{p}_j \partial z_j(p)/\partial p_i = 0$$

for each i. Using Walras' law it is straightforward to show that this is satisfied by $p = \bar{p}$. If it is also satisfied by some $p \neq \bar{p}$ then, just as in the proof of Proposition 3.6, $z_k > 0$ where k is the commodity whose price relative to the equilibrium is the largest; again using Walras' law we may show that this implies a contradiction. It follows that $\bar{p}z(p)$ has a unique minimum (of zero) at $\bar{p}$, and thus that $\bar{p}z(p) > 0$ for all $p \neq \bar{p}$. This means that the economy displays revealed preference; since it has a unique equilibrium it is therefore stable.

This approach relies on the 'Euclidean distance' Lyapounov function. The direct approach (which does not assume differentiability) uses the 'maximum absolute value' Lyapounov function.

Proposition 6.3 A substitutive economy is stable.

Proof Let p be the unique (from Proposition 3.6) equilibrium and define the Lyapounov function

$$V(p) = \max_i |p_i/\bar{p}_i - 1|.$$

Let k be the relevant maximiser and consider the case where $p_k > \bar{p}_k$; then, where we can differentiate,

$$\dot{V}(p) = \dot{p}_k/\bar{p}_k = z_k(p)/\bar{p}_k.$$

But, just as in the proof of Proposition 3.6, $z_k(p) < 0$ for all $p \neq \bar{p}$, so that $\dot{V} < 0$ and V is decreasing. The case where $p_k < \bar{p}_k$ is treated in an exactly parallel way. We can only not differentiate where the relevant maximum is attained by more than one commodity; it is not difficult to extend the argument to this case (see Problem 3).

It is worth noting that none of these conditions depends on the choice of numeraire or the units of measurement of commodities, or indeed on the differentiability of the excess demand function. If we permit the choice of numeraire to be material there is a further restriction ensuring stability, though a satisfactory definition of this requires the excess demand function to be differentiable. This is the condition of dominant diagonality, or that own price effects are negative and dominate all others, at least in some units of measurement. Formally, this requires that, at every p, $z_{ii} < 0$ and, for some fixed vector $c > 0$,

$$c_i|z_{ii}| > \Sigma_{j \neq i} c_j |z_{ij}| \quad (i, j < n).$$

Since a choice of units of measurement is involved it is clear that the original units are irrelevant. However, the choice of numeraire is important, for it is simple to construct an economy which has this property for one choice of numeraire but not for another. Note that this cannot be avoided by taking the sum in the inequality over all commodities including the numeraire, for this would contradict homogeneity.

The reason why this condition might be expected to ensure stability is that it is a relaxation of the extreme case where there are no cross-price effects: then each market is independently stable, as in the case discussed above where there was only one non-numeraire commodity. Stability is demonstrated formally using the Lyapounov function

$$V(p) = \max_i |z_i(p)/c_i|$$

where c_i is as in the definition. Let k be the relevant maximiser, and consider the case where $z_k > 0$; then, where we can differentiate,

$$\dot{V} = \Sigma_j z_{kj} \dot{p}_j = \Sigma_j z_{kj} z_j.$$

Using the definition of dominant diagonality for k, multipled by z_k, and noting that

$$c_j z_k \geq c_k |z_j|,$$

we have

$$c_k |z_{kk}| z_k > \Sigma_{j \neq k} c_j |z_{kj}| z_k$$
$$\geq \Sigma_{j \neq k} c_k |z_{kj}| |z_j| \geq \Sigma_{j \neq k} c_k z_{kj} z_j,$$

so that, noting that $z_{kk} < 0$,

$$-z_{kk}z_k > \Sigma_{j \neq k} z_{kj}z_j,$$

and therefore

$$\dot{V} = \Sigma_j z_{kj}z_j < 0.$$

The case where $z_k < 0$ is treated in an exactly parallel way, and the cases where the maximum is attained by more than one commodity, so we cannot differentiate, are treated as in Proposition 6.3. It follows that V is decreasing, and thus that equilibrium is stable.

6.4 LOCAL STABILITY

The reason for considering local stability is that it allows us to understand more generally the causes of stability or instability. Since

$$z = x - y - r$$

the Jacobian matrix Z of the excess demand function is the difference between the Jacobian X of the demand function and Y of the supply function. We consider the latter first. It was shown in Chapter 2 that for any distinct prices p and $\bar{p}$ we have

$$(p - \bar{p})(y(p) - y(\bar{p})) > 0;$$

since

$$y(p) - y(\bar{p}) = Y(p - \bar{p})$$

in the neighbourhood of the equilibrium $\bar{p}$ this means that

$$(p - \bar{p})Y(p - \bar{p}) > 0,$$

or that Y is positive definite. (In fact this was shown for individual supply functions, but carries over to the aggregate since the sum of positive definite matrices is positive definite.) It also follows from the discussion of Chapter 2 that the Jacobian X is the sum of the matrices X' of substitution effects and X'' of wealth effects, and that (if we apply the same argument as for Y) X' is negative definite. It follows that

$$Z = X' + X'' - Y$$

will be negative definite, and therefore stable, provided that X' is small: large wealth effects are the only reason for instability. This gives us a more general understanding of stability, particularly since we may have small wealth effects without revealed preference, substitutability, or diagonal dominance.

An example which shows this also shows another interesting property, that stability may depend on the choice of units. Note that revealed preference, substitutability, or diagonal dominance imply stability in any units, so an example of an economy whose stability depends on the choice of units must be an example of an economy which is stable, for the appropriate units, and therefore has small wealth effects, but does not have any of these three properties. As we have noted, an economy with two commodities (including numeraire) will always be stable if the non-numeraire commodity is normal. Formally, this is because the relevant matrix reduces to the negative slope of the excess demand function: clearly this is negative in any units. If there are three commodities then stability will depend on the units only if one non-numeraire commodity is normal and the other is not: if both are normal, equilibrium may or may not be stable and if neither are normal, equilibrium will always be unstable. This is easily seen by noting that a 2×2 matrix is stable if and only if its trace is negative and its determinant positive. Then the sign of the trace is affected by the choice of units only if diagonal elements differ in sign, while the sign of the determinant never depends on the units. With four or more commodities it is easy to construct examples where stability may depend on the choice of units (as well as on the choice of numeraire) even if all commodities are normal.

If we examine the dimensionality of the components of the matrix Z we may see that the effect of increasing the units of measurement of the commodities by the positive factors α_i ($i < n$) is that of replacing the non-numeraire Jacobian Z by DZ, where D is the positive diagonal matrix with components

$$d_{ii} = 1/\alpha_i^2 \ (i < n).$$

Thus, in general, an economy with non-numeraire Jacobian Z is unit-free stable if DZ is a stable matrix for all positive diagonal matrices D. The reason why stability may depend on units is essentially that units of measurement may be interpreted as speeds of adjustment: DZ is equivalently Z with speeds of adjustment D, in the sense that

$$\dot{p}_i = d_{ii}z_i(p).$$

It is quite natural that stability may depend on relative speeds of adjustment.

6.5 DYNAMIC EQUILIBRIUM

The dynamic equilibrium of Chapter 5 provides a link between the existence and stability discussions, since it incorporates an implicit dynamic structure and therefore does not require the explicit tatonnement. It is of interest to compare the stability of the competitive and dynamic equilibria, of course for comparable (exchange) economies, those of the forms (Π, R) and (Π, R, a) respectively, where R is a positive diagonal matrix.

To do this we must first compare the competitive and monopoly demand systems. The competitive demand for consumer i maximises his preference subject to his expenditure not exceeding $p_i r_i$, while his monopoly demand maximises his preferences subject to his expenditure not exceeding

$$\min \{a_i p_i^2, p_i r_i\}.$$

Thus if we confine our attention to the local region where demand is (approximately) linear the effect of a change in p_j on the competitive and monopoly demands for any consumer $i \neq j$ will be the same: the only difference between the two maximising problems is the level of wealth, which is not affected by the price change. A change in p_j may however affect the competitive and monopoly wealths of consumer j differently, and thus his demand changes, but in a 'large' economy his individual effect will be unnoticeable in the aggregate. Thus the slopes of the competitive and monopoly demand functions are approximately the same, so we may approximate the non-numeraire Jacobian X of the monopoly demand function by the Jacobian Z of the competitive excess demand function (since this is the same as the Jacobian of the competitive demand function in an exchange economy).

The dynamic process is implicit in the generating function defined in Chapter 5 by

$$f_i(p) = \max \{\tfrac{1}{2}(x_i(p)/a_i + p_i), (x_i(p) - r_i)/a_i + p_i\} \quad (i < n)$$

with $p_n \equiv 1$, where x is the monopoly demand function. In its continuous time form this may be written as

$$\dot{p}_i = \tfrac{1}{2}(x_i(p)/a_i - p_i) \text{ if } p_i < r_i/a_i,$$

$$\dot{p}_i = (x_i(p) - r_i)/a_i \text{ if } p_i \geq r_i/a_i$$

for $i < n$, with $p_n \equiv 1$. In the case where $p_i \geq r_i/a_i$ for each i, this immediately reduces to

$$\dot{p} = DX(p - \bar{p})$$

in the neighbourhood of the equilibrium $\bar{p}$, where D is a positive diagonal matrix with elements $d_{ii} = a_i$. Since we are approximating X by Z this is to say that the unit-free stability of X, or of the dynamic equilibrium, is equivalent to that of Z, or of the competitive equilibrium. In the other extreme case where $p_i < r_i/a_i$ for each i, we have

$$\dot{p} = \tfrac{1}{2}(DX - I)(p - \bar{p})$$

(where I is the unit matrix), so that equilibrium is stable if and only if $\frac{1}{2}(DX - I)$ is a stable matrix, or equivalently if and only if $DZ - I$ is. Now assume Z to be unit-free stable, so that CDZ is stable for any positive diagonal matrix C: then the real part of each characteristic root of $C(DZ - I)$ is smaller (by at least an amount equal to the smallest diagonal element of C) than the real part of the corresponding characteristic root of CDZ, and therefore negative. It follows that $DZ - I$ is unit-free stable. However the unit-free stability of $DZ - I$ does not imply that of DZ, as may easily be seen by example. Thus in this sense the dynamic equilibrium is more stable than the competitive. Of course this is only in the linear or local case in a large economy, and ignores what may happen when p_i exceeds r_i/a_i for some i and falls short of this for others.

Notes
1 The general stability problem is summarised by T. Negishi [The Stability of a Competitive Economy: A Survey Article, *Econometrica*, 1962] where a wider concept of stability is employed which does not require uniqueness: an economy is quasi-stable if all limit points of solution paths are equilibria, so the economy may only tend to the set of equilibria rather than tend to one of these. Of course if equilibria are separated (or if equilibrium is unique) this is the same as stability.
2 We have considered revealed preference and substitutability as independent in general, though shown that the latter implies the former in the differentiable case. In fact this argument may be extended to the general case, as it is by H. Nikaido [*Convex Structures and Economic Theory*, New York, 1968]. Moreover, as with uniqueness, substitutability may be weakened to weak substitutability with connectedness, as is shown by K. J. Arrow and F. H. Hahn [*General Competitive Analysis*, San Francisco, 1971].
3 Stability of competitive equilibrium may also be shown under more realistic dynamic structures than the tatonnement. Such non-tatonnement schemes, allowing trade out of equilibrium, are discussed by Negishi and by Arrow and Hahn.

Problems
1 Show that the functions

$$V(p) = (p - \bar{p})(p - \bar{p}),$$
$$V'(p) = \max_i |p_i/\bar{p}_i - 1|,$$
$$V''(p) = \max_i |z_i(p)|,$$

where $\bar{p}$ is the unique equilibrium price, are Lyapounov functions.

2. Complete the demonstration that substitutability implies revealed preference in the differentiable case.
3. In the proof of Proposition 6.3 show that V is decreasing where the relevant maximum is attained by more than one commodity.
4. Show that diagonal dominance for all commodities including the numeraire, that is

$$c_i|z_{ii}| > \Sigma_{j \neq i} c_j |z_{ij}| \quad (i, j = 1, \ldots n)$$

is impossible (for any $c > 0$).

5. Construct an economy which has diagonal dominance for one numeraire but not for another.
6. Show that a 2×2 matrix is stable if and only if its trace is negative and its determinant is positive, and thus that a three-commodity economy where exactly one non-numeraire commodity is normal is always locally stable for some choice of units of measurement and unstable for others.
7. Construct a four-commodity economy with all commodities normal where stability may depend on the units of measurement.
8. Construct a stable matrix A such that $A - I$ is unstable (thus illustrating that the unit-free stability of the dynamic equilibrium does not imply that of the competitive).

7 Comparative Statics

The preceding chapter examined the conditions under which the economy would tend to some new equilibrium when disturbed from its original equilibrium. We now examine the properties of this new equilibrium, that is investigate how the equilibrium of an economy depends on its parameters. Formally, the analysis is quite similar to the preceding stability analysis, which is appropriate since it is not very useful to answer the comparative static question without the stability one, and indeed the latter may help with the former. We continue to use the excess demand representation of the economy, and interpret all prices as numeraire prices. Again we concentrate on the competitive equilibrium, and then relate this to the dynamic equilibrium.

7.1 PARAMETER CHANGES

The basic question we consider is, given some change in the parameters of the economy, that is in preferences, resources, shares, or production possibilities, how the equilibrium changes. Such questions are the essence of positive economics, since they generate meaningful theorems, that is propositions which are open to possible empirical refutation. Thus the normative statement that an equilibrium is an optimum is unverifiable empirically, unlike the positive claim that an increase in demand leads to an increase in price.

The basic parameter change we consider is that which is embodied in a demand increase, or equivalently a supply decrease, for some single commodity at the original equilibrium price, with the excess demand functions for all other non-numeraire commodities unaltered. Of course the excess demand function for the numeraire must then change, this change being dictated by Walras' law. More complex parameter changes may be considered in terms of components of this simple form. The effect of the demand change which we consider is that on price, that is on the competitive equilibrium numeraire price.

Definition There is a demand increase for commodity $i < n$ in an economy z with equilibrium $\bar{p}$ when z is replaced by z' such that

$$z'_i(\bar{p}) > z_i(\bar{p}),$$

$$z'_j(p) \equiv z_j(p) \quad (i \neq j < n).$$

It is clear that the laws of comparative statics will depend on the properties of the economy, for example whether it is substitutive or not, but there is one basic result we should expect to hold in any 'regular' economy: this is that an increase in demand for some commodity would raise the price of that commodity. However, this does not hold in general, though it does apply to all revealed preference economies.

Proposition 7.1 If there is a demand increase for some commodity in a revealed preference economy then the price of this commodity increases.

Proof Let $\bar{p}$ and $\bar{p}'$ be old and new equilibria, and, in the definition of a demand increase, let

$$z'_1(\bar{p}) > z_1(\bar{p}),$$

$$z'_i(p) \equiv z_i(p) \ (1 < i < n).$$

Then noting that $z_i(\bar{p}) = 0$ $(1 < i < n)$ and $p_n = 1$ revealed preference gives

$$\bar{p}'z'(\bar{p}) = \bar{p}'_1 z'_1(\bar{p}) + z'_n(\bar{p}) > 0.$$

Further, Walras' law gives

$$\bar{p}z'(\bar{p}) = \bar{p}_1 z'_1(\bar{p}) + z'_n(\bar{p}) = 0,$$

so on subtracting we have

$$(\bar{p}'_1 - \bar{p}_1)z'_1(\bar{p}) > 0,$$

or, as $z'_1(\bar{p}) > 0$, $\bar{p}'_1 > \bar{p}_1$.

An interesting aspect of this result is that it does not require equilibrium to be unique: whatever old and new equilibria $\bar{p}$ and $\bar{p}'$ are chosen we have $\bar{p}'_1 > \bar{p}_1$. However, if we consider the change in more detail, for example the prices of the other commodities, it is plausible that we might have the new price exceeding the old for one pair of equilibria, and the reverse for another. This means that in order to obtain more determinate results it will be helpful to restrict our attention to economies where the old and new equilibria are unique.

COMPARATIVE STATICS

7.2 SUBSTITUTABILITY

One restriction on the economy which ensures that equilibrium is unique (and stable) is substitutability; it transpires that this is also a powerful restriction for comparative statics. Of course a differentiable substitutive economy displays revealed preference, so it follows from Proposition 7.1 that if the demand for a commodity increases in this case then so does its price. However, in a substitutive economy this price increase would bring about an increase in the demands for all other commodities so, applying Proposition 7.1 to these, we might expect their prices to rise as well. In fact this applies even without differentiability.

Proposition 7.2 If there is a demand increase for some commodity in a substitutive economy then all prices increase.

Proof Let
$$z_1'(\bar{p}) > z_1(\bar{p}),$$
$$z_i'(p) \equiv z_i(p) \quad (1 < i < n)$$

as in Proposition 7.1, and define
$$a = \max_i \bar{p}_i/\bar{p}_i' = \bar{p}_k/\bar{p}_k',$$

say. Now if $a \geq 1$ then $a\bar{p}_k' = \bar{p}_k$ and $a\bar{p}_i' > \bar{p}_i$ ($i \neq k$), so that substitutability and homogeneity give
$$0 = z_k'(a\bar{p}') = z_k'(a\bar{p}_1', \ldots a\bar{p}_{n-1}', a) > z_k'(\bar{p}_1, \ldots \bar{p}_{n-1}, 1) = z_k'(\bar{p}).$$

Since
$$z_1'(\bar{p}) > z_1(\bar{p}) = 0,$$
$$z_i(\bar{p}) = z_i(\bar{p}) = 0 \; (i > 1)$$

this is a contradiction, so we must have $a < 1$, or $\bar{p}_i' > \bar{p}_i$ for each i. (This assumes $\max_i \bar{p}_i/\bar{p}_i'$ to be attained uniquely, but the general case follows in the same way; see Problem 2.)

Since the intuitive reasoning behind this proposition is that the original increase in demand leads, in effect, to secondary increases in demand for the other commodities, we might expect these secondary effects to be smaller than the original effect, so that the proportional price increases are smaller.

Proposition 7.3 If there is a demand increase for some commodity in a substitutive economy then the price of this commodity increases proportionately more than that of any other commodity.

Proof Proceed as in Proposition 7.2, but define
$$\beta = \min_i \bar{p}_i/\bar{p}'_i = \bar{p}_j/\bar{p}'_j,$$
say; clearly
$$\beta \leq \alpha < 1.$$
Then in parallel with Proposition 7.2 substitutability and homogeneity give $z'_j(\bar{p}) > 0$. Since $z'_1(\bar{p}) > 0$ and $z'_i(\bar{p}) = 0$ for $i > 1$ this means that $j = 1$, so that
$$\bar{p}'_1/\bar{p}_1 > \bar{p}'_i/\bar{p}_i \quad (i > 1).$$
These results, that an increase in the demand for some commodity leads to an increase in its price, to an increase in the prices of all other commodities, and to a larger proportional increase for its price than for the others, are known as the three Hicksian laws.

It may happen that an initial demand change will lead to further demand changes, for example the demand increase for one commodity may bring about a supply change for some second commodity which makes the price of the second commodity return to its original level. This may be interpreted in terms of the 'short run' and the 'long run'. The formal analysis may for example be interpreted as being short-run, that is not allowing certain aspects of supply (the stimulation of new inventions) time to take effect; in the long run these aspects do take effect, for example by increasing the supply of some second commodity so as to return its price to its original level. (However, there is no formal distinction in the analysis between the short and long run.) We show that, in this sense, short-run effects are greater than long-run; this proposition is known as the le Chatelier principle.

Proposition 7.4 If there is a demand increase for some commodity in a substitutive economy then the prices of all commodities increase less if the supply of some second commodity is adjusted so that its price is unchanged than if this is not adjusted.

Proof Let $\bar{p}$, $\bar{p}'$, and $\bar{p}''$ be the equilibria before the demand increase for commodity 1, after the increase when the supply of commodity 2 is not adjusted, and after the increase when this is adjusted. From Proposition 7.2 we have $\bar{p}' > \bar{p}$, so that the supply of commodity 2 must be increased to make $\bar{p}''_2 = \bar{p}_2$ (otherwise
$$\bar{p}''_2 \geq \bar{p}'_2 > \bar{p}_2,$$
from Proposition 7.2). Since this is equivalent to a demand decrease, it follows from the same proposition that $\bar{p}'' < \bar{p}'$.

We have so far been concerned with the effects of an increase in demand in some given economy. It is also of interest to compare these effects with the corresponding effects when the economy itself has been changed in some given way. For example, if the excess demand function for some commodity were steeper, so that the commodity were more normal, then we might expect the effects of some given demand increase to be smaller: this is obvious in the simple case where there is only one non-numeraire commodity. As a second example, if there were more substitutability between some commodity and another then we might expect the effects of some given increase in demand to be larger: substitutability ensures that all prices increase, and it is plausible that they do this more the more substitutability there is. We demonstrate both these propositions.

Where the economy z is differentiable, commodity i, or by extension the economy, becomes more normal if $-z_{ii}$ increases (note that $z_{ii} < 0$ in a substitutive economy because of Walras' law). Similarly, commodities i and k, or the economy, become more substitutive if z_{ik} increases. Thus we would investigate changes in both diagonal and offdiagonal elements of the matrix Z. In the general case the definitions are simply the finite forms of these, illustrated in Figures 7.1 and 7.2 respectively.

Definition An economy z with unique equilibrium $\bar{p}$ becomes more normal if z is replaced by $\tilde{z}$ where, for some $i < n$,

$$\tilde{z}_i(p) < (or >) z_i(p)$$

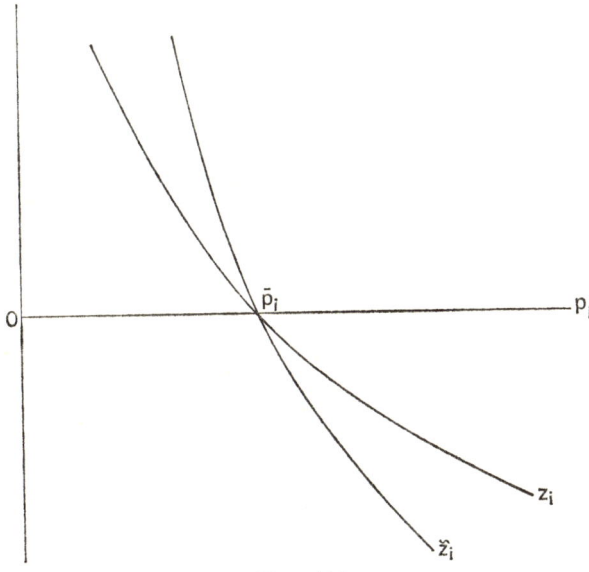

Fig. 7.1

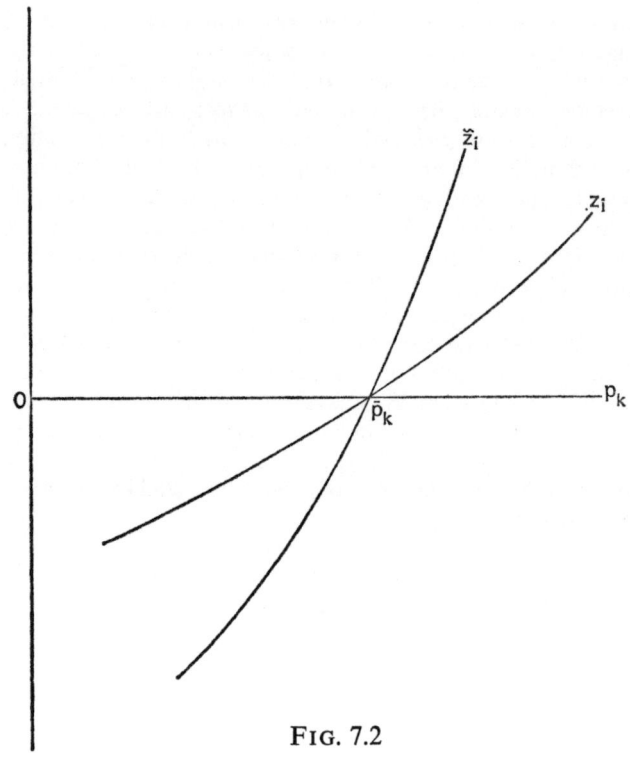

Fig. 7.2

whenever $p_i > (or <) \bar{p}_i$, and

$$\tilde{z}_j(p) \equiv z_j(p) \ (i \neq j < n);$$

it becomes more substitutive if z is replaced by $\tilde{z}$ where, for some distinct $i, k < n$,

$$\tilde{z}_i(p) > (or <) z_i(p)$$

whenever $p_k > (or <) \bar{p}_k$, and

$$\tilde{z}_j(p) \equiv z_j(p) \ (i \neq j < n).$$

Note that the excess demand for the numeraire is not specified explicitly, since again this must exactly compensate the other changes, and also that, because of continuity, we have

$$\tilde{z}_i(p) = z_i(p)$$

when $p_i = \bar{p}_i$ (for normality) or when $p_k = \bar{p}_k$ (for substitutability).

Proposition 7.5 If a substitutive economy becomes more normal then the effects of a demand increase on all prices are reduced.

COMPARATIVE STATICS

Proof Let z and z' (with equilibria $\bar{p}$ and $\bar{p}'$) be the original economies before and after the demand increase, with $\tilde{z}$ and $\tilde{z}'$ (with equilibria $\tilde{p}$ and $\tilde{p}'$) the corresponding modified economies (after commodity i becomes more normal). Then from Proposition 7.2 we have $\bar{p}' > \bar{p}$ and
$$\tilde{p}' > \tilde{p} = \bar{p};$$
in particular $\tilde{p}'_i > \bar{p}_i$, so by definition
$$\tilde{z}_i(\bar{p}') < z_i(\bar{p}'),$$
and therefore
$$\tilde{z}'_i(\bar{p}') < z'_i(\bar{p}').$$
Since
$$\tilde{z}'_j(p) \equiv z'_j(p) \quad (j \neq i)$$
this means that z' is obtained from $\tilde{z}'$ simply by a demand increase for commodity i, so again using Proposition 7.2 we have
$$\bar{p}' > \tilde{p}' > \bar{p}$$
as required.

Proposition 7.6 If a substitutive economy becomes more substitutive then the effects of a demand increase on all prices are magnified.

Proof The proof is exactly parallel to Proposition 7.5, only now $\tilde{p}'_i > \bar{p}_i$ implies that
$$\tilde{z}_k(\bar{p}') > z_k(\bar{p}')$$
so that z' is obtained from $\tilde{z}'$ by a demand decrease for commodity k, and thus
$$\bar{p}' > \tilde{p}' > \bar{p}.$$

These two propositions, that normality increases and substitutability decreases the flexibility of the economy, are known as the fourth and fifth Hicksian laws.

7.3 HICKSIAN CROSS

It is helpful to consider a simple geometric representation of the preceding five propositions known as the Hicksian Cross; this is illustrated in Figure 7.3. We consider a three-commodity differentiable substitutive economy z with commodity 3 as numeraire; note that $z_{ii} < 0$ and $z_{ij} > 0$ ($i \neq j$). Then for any given p_2 (with $p_3 = 1$) there is some p_1 which makes
$$z_1(p_1, p_2, 1) = 0,$$
that is, brings the market for commodity 1 into equilibrium; denote this by $\varphi(p_2)$. Since
$$z_{11} dp_1 + z_{12} dp_2 = 0$$

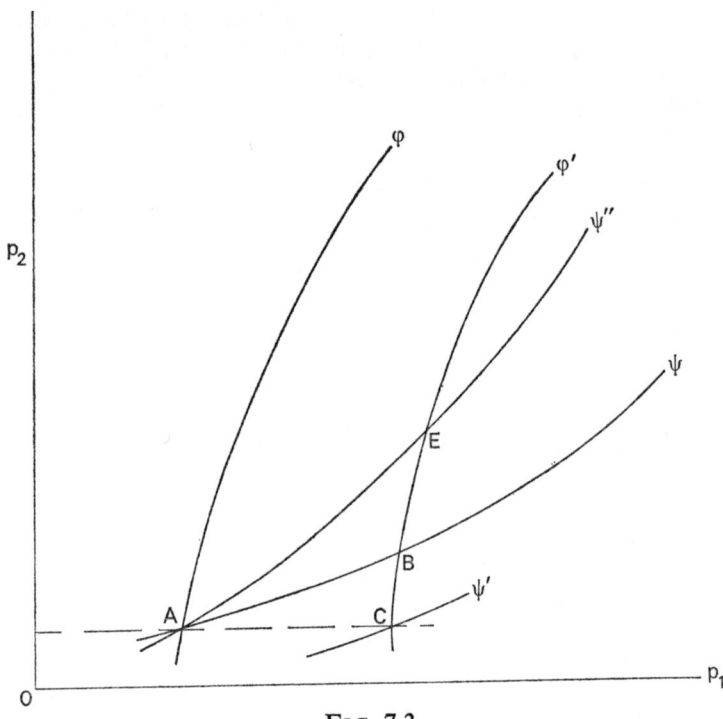

Fig. 7.3

at equilibrium it is clear that

$$d\varphi/dp_2 = dp_1/dp_2 = -z_{12}/z_{11} > 0,$$

so the locus $p_1 = \varphi(p_2)$ is the upward-sloping curve φ in the figure. In the same way the locus of the p_2 which makes

$$z_2(p_1, p_2, 1) = 0$$

for given p_1 is the upward-sloping curve ψ; note that this must be above φ for low values of p_1. The point A at which these two curves intersect is identified with the equilibrium $(\bar{p}_1, \bar{p}_2, 1)$, for there

$$z_1 = z_2 = 0$$

and so $z_3 = 0$ by Walras' law. At this point it is straightforward to show that $d \log p_2 < d \log p_1$ on the curve φ and $d \log p_1 < d \log p_2$ on ψ.

Now consider a demand increase for commodity 1. Then the curve φ will shift to φ', so the new equilibrium is identified with the

COMPARATIVE STATICS 91

point B. It is clear from the figure that p_1 is higher at B (the first Hicksian law), that p_2 is higher (the second law), and that p_1 has increased (proportionately) more than p_2 (the third law). Next let the supply of commodity 2 be adjusted so that its price is not changed. Then ψ shifts to ψ' and the new equilibrium is C. Clearly p_1 has increased less from A to C than from A to B (the le Chatelier principle). Finally, assume that either commodity 2 becomes less normal, so that $-z_{22}$ decreases, or that commodities 2 and 1 become more substitutive, so that z_{21} increases. In both cases

$$-z_{21}/z_{22} = d\psi/dp_1$$

increases, so that ψ shifts to ψ'' and the new equilibrium is E. Clearly both prices have increased more from A to E than from A to B (the fourth or fifth Hicksian law).

7.4 CORRESPONDENCE PRINCIPLE

It was noted in Chapter 6 that an egg standing on its head, or an economy at an unstable equilibrium, would seldom be observed. This suggests that we may reverse the argument of Chapter 6, and instead of considering what attributes of the economy ensure its stability, assume the economy to be stable and consider what information, particularly comparative static information, this implies. The existence of such implications is known as the correspondence principle.

We consider only local effects, and as in Chapter 6 represent the economy z in the neighbourhood of equilibrium by its non-numeraire Jacobian matrix Z. It is helpful now to consider a demand increase for some commodity i as being embodied in some parameter a, in the sense that p is an equilibrium for this parameter value if $z(p; a) = 0$. Then differentiating gives the comparative static system

$$Z dp = b$$

where b is the vector $-(\partial z_i/\partial a)da$. However, since a is chosen so as to increase the demand for commodity i (when increased), and effect the demand for no other commodity, we have $b_i < 0$ and $b_j = 0$ $(j \neq i)$.

We enquire then what the stability of Z implies about $Z^{-1}b$ (it does of course imply that Z^{-1} exists, noting Problem 8, Chapter 1). In its weak form this is not much, but if we strengthen the assumption to unit-free stability we have a basic result resembling Proposition 7.1.

Proposition 7.7 Locally, if there is a demand increase for some commodity in a unit-free stable economy then the price of this commodity does not decrease.

Proof If DZ is stable then

$$\Sigma_i(Z^{-1}D^{-1})_{ii} = \Sigma_i a_{ii}/d_{ii} < 0$$

where $A = Z^{-1}$, by the Routh–Hurwitz theorem. If this applies for all $d_{ii} > 0$ then we must have each $a_{ii} \leq 0$; then solving

$$Z dp = b$$

where $b_i < 0$ and $b_j = 0$ $(j \neq i)$ gives

$$dp_i = b_i a_{ii} \geq 0,$$

as required.

Note that the price may not change at all, though it is easy to see that for at least one choice of i it will strictly increase.

We return to the original correspondence principle by considering what restrictions must be made to the matrix Z to ensure that its stability implies definite comparative static knowledge, that is knowledge of the signs of each component of the vector $Z^{-1}b$. Since we seek sign or qualitative knowledge we naturally consider qualitative restrictions, that is restrictions on the signs of the components of the matrix Z. By the sign of an element we mean whether it is positive or negative; for simplicity we exclude the boundary case of its being zero. We also restrict our attention to economies where all commodities are normal, and where there are at least three non-numeraire commodities; the small dimension cases are easily analysed directly.

We have

$$dp_i = b_i Z_{ij}/|Z|$$

where Z_{ij} is the cofactor of z_{ij} in Z and $|Z|$ the determinant of Z. Then since the Routh–Hurwitz theorem implies that the determinant $|Z|$ has sign $(-1)^{n-1}$ the problem of signing dp_j reduces to that of signing the cofactor Z_{ij}. But this is the determinant of an $(n-2) \times (n-2)$ matrix, which when evaluated may be seen to include the terms $-z_{ij}Mz_{kk}$ and $z_{jk}z_{ki}M$, where i, j, and k are distinct and M is the product of all the diagonal elements of Z except z_{ii}, z_{jj} and z_{kk}. It is clear that the diagonal elements may be made arbitrarily large in absolute value without violating the stability assumption, so we may always choose numerical values such that these two terms dominate all others in Z_{ij}; then the sign of Z_{ij} will only be determinate if the signs of these two terms are the same. Since we assume z_{kk} to be negative this is equivalent to the condition that the sign of z_{ji} be the same as that of $z_{jk}z_{ki}$, or equivalently that

$$z_{ji}z_{jk}z_{ki} > 0.$$

It is easy to see that this condition implies that z_{ij} and z_{ji} both have the same sign, so we may unambiguously label the pair of commodities i and j as substitutes (if this is positive) or complements (if negative). The condition then implies that substitutes of substitutes and complements of complements are substitutes, while substitutes of complements and complements of substitutes are complements. In this form the condition is known as the Hicksian chain rule, a rule which of course need only hold for the non-numeraire commodities. Only in normal economies with this property is the correspondence principle helpful.

Now that we know in which economies the correspondence principle is fruitful we can consider what it implies. First, however, it is helpful to give an equivalent characterisation of the Hicksian chain rule known as the Morishima property. This is that there are two sets of non-numeraire commodities, R and S, such that z_{ij} is positive if i and j belong to the same set and negative if they belong to different sets. To see that this characterisation is implied by the Hicksian chain rule we proceed inductively, and assume this implication to hold for $m-1$ commodities. Then with m commodities we have $z_{im}z_{mi} > 0$ for each $i < m$; also if $i \in R$ (or S) and $z_{im} > 0$ then $z_{jm} > 0$ for each $j \in R$ (or S) so that $m \in R$ (or S), while if $i \in R$ (or S) and $z_{im} < 0$ then $z_{jm} < 0$ for each $j \in R$ (or S) so that $m \in S$ (or R). Thus the implication holds for m commodities; since it clearly holds for three non-numeraire commodities it therefore holds for an arbitrary number. The converse of this, that the Morishima property implies the Hicksian chain rule, is obvious.

Definition Locally, an economy Z has the Morishima property if, for some sets $R, S \subset \{1, \ldots n-1\}$, $z_{ij} > 0$ if $i, j \in R$ or $i, j \in S$ ($i \neq j$), while $z_{ij} < 0$ if $i \in R, j \in S$ or $i \in S, j \in R$.

It is clear that this is a generalisation of substitutability, since it reduces to this if either R or S is empty. However, it still implies some real restriction: for example, it admits an economy with coffee, tea, cream, and milk as commodities, but does not allow one with coffee, cream, whisky, and soda (which in fact obeys the reverse of the Hicksian chain rule). Unlike substitutability, the Morishima property does not cover the numeraire, and also unlike substitutability it does not ensure stability (so the assumption of stability made by the correspondence principle is a real restriction).

We may now consider the specific comparative statical laws implied by stability. Since the economy has complements the informal reasoning behind Proposition 7.2 will no longer apply, and we should not expect a demand increase for some commodity to lead to an increase in the prices of all commodities. However, reasoning in a parallel way we should expect the prices of the affected commodity and its substitutes to rise, and the prices of its complements to fall.

Proposition 7.8 Locally, if there is a demand increase for some commodity in a stable Morishima economy then the prices of this commodity and its substitutes increase and the prices of its complements decrease.

Proof First note that Z is similar to a matrix with positive off-diagonal elements, for if D is a diagonal matrix with $d_{ii} = 1$ if $i \in R$ and $d_{ii} = -1$ if $i \in S$ (in the definition of the Morishima property) then in

$$A = DZD^{-1}$$

we have each $a_{ij} > 0$ ($i \neq j$). Then if

$$a > \max_i |a_{ii}|$$

we may write

$$A = B - aI$$

where B is a positive matrix. Now (noting Problem 7, Chapter 1) if λ is a characteristic root of Z then it is also a root of A, and therefore

$$\mu = \lambda + a$$

is a root of B. But the Frobenius theorem ensures that B has a real positive maximal root, say,

$$\mu^* = \lambda^* + a$$

and since Z is stable its roots have negative real parts, so that $\lambda^* < 0$, and $a > \mu^*$. Then from the Frobenius theorem

$$A^{-1} = (B-aI)^{-1}$$

is a negative matrix, so in

$$C = Z^{-1} = D^{-1}A^{-1}D$$

we have $c_{ij} < 0$ if $i,j \in R$ or $i,j \in S$ or $i = j$ (that is if $z_{ij} > 0$ or $i = j$) with $c_{ij} > 0$ if $i \in R, j \in S$ or $i \in S, j \in R$ (that is if $z_{ij} < 0$). Since $dp_i = c_{i1}b_1$ and $b_1 < 0$ (assuming the demand increase to be for commodity 1), the conclusion follows.

Thus in the Morishima case the correspondence principle gives complete comparative static information, though this is the only case where it does this.

7.5 DYNAMIC EQUILIBRIUM

We have so far considered only the comparative statics of the competitive equilibrium; it is also of interest to consider parallel questions for the dynamic equilibrium. However, for the questions we have asked, this only involves a reinterpretation since we again examine the comparative statics of the equilibrium $\bar{p}$ of a system z given by $z(\bar{p}) = 0$. The only difference is that z is now the monopolistic rather than the competitive excess demand function.

There is however one aspect of the dynamic equilibrium which has no counterpart in the competitive framework. This is a change in the (downward) slope of some perceived demand curve, a_i; if this increases then the commodity is perceived to be more price responsive, or competitive. As shown in Chapter 6, the relevant equilibrium condition for the dynamic equilibrium is

$$0 = f_i(p) = \tfrac{1}{2}(x_i(p)/a_i - p_i) \text{ if } p_i < r_i/a_i,$$
$$0 = f_i(p) = (x_i(p) - r_i)/a_i \text{ if } p_i \geqq r_i/a_i.$$

Differentiating and rearranging gives

$$dp_i/da_i = -h_{ii}\partial f_i/\partial a_i$$

where H is the inverse of the Jacobian of f. It follows exactly as in Proposition 7.7 that if equilibrium is unit-free stable then $h_{ii} < 0$; it is also clear that

$$\partial f_i/\partial a_i = -\tfrac{1}{2}x_i/a_i^2 < 0 \text{ if } p_i < r_i/a_i,$$
$$\partial f_i/\partial a_i = 0 \text{ if } p_i \geqq r_i/a_i.$$

Thus $dp_i/da_i \leqq 0$, and an increase in the competitiveness of a commodity cannot cause its price to rise.

Notes

1 The local comparative statics framework is that of J. R. Hicks [*Value and Capital*, Oxford, 1946], who demonstrated the first three Hicksian laws and suggested the remaining two, and of P. A. Samuelson [*Foundations of Economic Analysis*, Cambridge (Mass.) 1947] who demonstrated the le Chatelier principle and proposed the correspondence principle. The approach for the global analysis considered here is that developed by M. Morishima [*Equilibrium, Stability and Growth*, Oxford, 1964], who also demonstrates a more general form of the le Chatelier principle.

2 Further aspects of the qualitative analysis of comparative statics and stability are discussed by M. G. Allingham and M. Morishima [Qualitative Economics and Comparative Statics, Chapter 1 in

Theory of Demand, Oxford, 1973], who also develop comparative static laws for economies which are not necessarily substitutive, such as those with the Morishima property (for which also see Problem 8). An alternative generalisation considers the effects of more complex parameter changes than simple demand increases; this is discussed by K. J. Arrow and F. H. Hahn [*General Competitive Analysis*, San Francisco, 1971].

Problems
1. Construct an economy where a demand increase for some commodity causes its price to fall, and show that this economy does not display revealed preference.
2. Complete the proof of Proposition 7.2 in the case where $\max_i \bar{p}_i/\bar{p}'_i$ is attained by more than one commodity.
3. Construct a stable economy where a demand increase for some commodity leaves its price unchanged.
4. Show that the correspondence principle always implies complete comparative static information in an economy with less than three non-numeraire commodities.
5. In a matrix Z show that

$$z_{ji}z_{jk}z_{ki} > 0$$

for each distinct i, j, k implies that $z_{ij}z_{ji} > 0$ for each distinct i, j.
6. Show that the Morishima property implies the Hicksian chain rule; also show that these are equivalent in an economy with three non-numeraire commodities.
7. Construct an unstable Morishima economy.
8. In a differentiable economy, where Proposition 7.8 will hold globally by repetition, formulate and prove results corresponding to Propositions 7.5 and 7.6 where substitutability is replaced by the Morishima property with stability.

Appendix: Social Preference

Appendix: Social Preference

General equilibrium theory has many normative, or optimality, aspects. The theory interprets such optimality in the sense of the Pareto social preference relation, which specifies that one state is socially preferred to another if some individual prefers the first and no one prefers the second, and that the two states are socially indifferent if neither is socially preferred. This of course involves value judgements, and unavoidably so. The purpose of this appendix is to provide an axiomatic basis for this interpretation; this is done in a more general framework than that of general equilibrium theory.

A.1 SOCIAL CHOICE

We consider a society consisting of a finite set N of individuals (indexed by $i = 1, \ldots n$) which must choose an alternative from an arbitrary set S of social states. To avoid trivialities we assume that there are at least two individuals and at least three states, and that no individual is indifferent between all states. For example, N may be the set of consumers and S the set of feasible consumption allocations, but no such 'economic' restriction is required. Each individual (i) has some preference ordering $\tilde{\pi}^i$ on S, with the associated strict preference and indifference relations π^i and $\sim^i$. The problem is to combine these individual preference relations to obtain a social preference relation $\tilde{\pi}$ (together with the derived relations π and $\sim$), or in other words to specify a preference aggregation function f which determines a relation $\tilde{\pi} = f(\Pi)$ on the set of states for every logically possible array $\Pi = (\tilde{\pi}^1, \ldots \tilde{\pi}^n)$ of individual preference orderings. Note that for the time being we do not require the social preference relation to be an ordering (that is to be complete, reflexive and transitive).

We have already implied some value judgement, albeit reasonable, in requiring social preference to depend on individual preference at all, but given this there would appear to be three absolutely minimal requirements for the aggregation function to be acceptable. Firstly, it should respect unanimity, in that, for two states x and y, x should be socially preferred to y if no one prefers y to x and someone actually prefers x to y. Secondly, the function should be impersonal, in that if some individual is weakly decisive over all pairs of states (in the sense that y cannot be socially preferred to x if this individual prefers x to y) then all individuals should have this status. Thirdly, social choice should be independent of irrelevant alternatives, in that the social preference between x and y should depend only on individual preferences between x and y. An aggregation function which has these properties is a social choice function.

Definition A social choice function f specifies a relation $\tilde{\pi} = f(\Pi)$ on S for every array $\Pi = (\tilde{\pi}^1, \ldots \tilde{\pi}^n)$ of orderings on S such that, for every $x, y \in S$: (1) $x\pi y$ whenever $x\tilde{\pi}^i y$ for each i with strict preference for some, while $x \sim y$ whenever $x \sim^i y$ for each i; (2) if there is some i such that $x\tilde{\pi} y$ whenever $x\pi^i y$, then $x\tilde{\pi} y$ whenever there is some j such that $x\pi^j y$; (3) if, when $\tilde{\pi}' = f(\Pi')$, $x\tilde{\pi}'^i y$ whenever $x\tilde{\pi}^i y$ for each i then $x\tilde{\pi}' y$ whenever $x\tilde{\pi} y$.

Examples of potential social choice functions are the two 'political' extremes of dictatorship, where, for two states x and y, x is socially preferred to y whenever it is preferred by some given individual (the dictator), and democracy, where x is socially preferred to y whenever it is preferred by the majority of individuals. There is also the 'economic' Pareto function, where x is socially preferred to y whenever x is preferred by some individual and y by none (and x is socially indifferent to y if neither state is socially preferred to the other).

Definition The Pareto social choice function specifies $x\tilde{\pi} y$ unless $y\tilde{\pi}^i x$ for each i with strict preference for some.

However, of these three examples it is clear that dictatorship does not qualify as it contradicts impersonality: if individual i is the dictator then he is weakly decisive, so that all individuals would have to be weakly decisive, and thus if $x\pi^i y$ and $y\pi^j x$ we would require $x\pi y$ and $y\tilde{\pi} x$, which is impossible. On the other hand, democracy and the Pareto rule do qualify, but may not be very useful since the relations they specify are not transitive: it is straightforward to see that democracy, but not the Pareto rule, may give

$$x\pi y \pi z \pi x,$$

while the Pareto rule may give

$$x \sim y \sim z \pi x.$$

Since the individual preference relations we start with are orderings it would be appropriate if the social preference relation we obtain were also an ordering, but this is not essential. The more basic

APPENDIX: SOCIAL PREFERENCE   101

requirement is that the social preference relation should be effective in the sense of determining a best state (not necessarily unique) from any non-empty finite set of states; here a state $x \in T \subset S$ is best in T according to the relation $\bar{\pi}$ if $x\bar{\pi}y$ for every $y \in T$.

It is clear that an ordering will be effective, for if $T = \{x_1, \ldots x_m\}$ we need only define $y_1 = x_1$ and $y_i = x_i$ if $x_i \pi y_{i-1}$ with $y_i = y_{i-1}$ otherwise ($i > 1$), so that y_m will be best in T. However, a relation which is not complete or not reflexive will not be effective: if x and y are not comparable then $\{x, y\}$ has no best state, while if x is not related to itself then $\{x\}$ has no best state. On the other hand, transitivity is not necessary for a relation to be effective: if

$$x \sim y \sim z \pi x$$

and we have reflexivity then z is best in $\{x, y, z\}, \{x, z\}, \{y, z\}$ and $\{z\}$, y is best in $\{x, y\}$ and $\{y\}$, and x is best in $\{x\}$.

A quasi-ordering, that is a relation $\bar{\pi}$ which is complete, reflexive, and quasi-transitive ($x\pi z$ whenever $x\pi y$ and $y\pi z$), is also effective. Assume that $\{x_1, \ldots x_k\}$ has a best state x_j. Then in $\{x_1, \ldots x_{k+1}\}$ either $x_j \bar{\pi} x_{k+1}$, in which case x_j is still best, or $x_{k+1} \pi x_j$: but then $x_{k+1} \bar{\pi} x_i$ for each $i < k + 1$ by quasi-transitivity, so that $\{x_1, \ldots x_{k+1}\}$ has a best state. Since $\{x_1\}$ obviously has a best state it follows by induction that any finite set has. (Note that quasi-transitivity implies that $x\bar{\pi}z$ whenever $x\pi y$ and $y \sim z$.) An example where quasi-transitivity might be relevant is where x is in fact worse than y but imperceptibly so, so that $x \sim y$, and likewise for y and z, but between x and z the difference becomes perceptible, so that $z\pi x$. Note that we cannot weaken transitivity further to require only that $x\bar{\pi}z$ whenever $x\pi y$ and $y\pi z$ and still retain effectiveness, for $\{w, x, y, z\}$ has no best state if

$$w\pi x\pi y\pi z\pi w$$

and $w \sim y$ with $x \sim z$.

We only require that the relation should determine a best state from any finite set since not even an ordering need do this from an infinite set: if $x_{i+1}\pi x_i$ for each i then $\{x_1, x_2, \ldots\}$ has no best state. Also, since we start with individual orderings we cannot expect to obtain a stronger social relation than an ordering.

A.2 DECISIVENESS

A set of individuals (or a single individual) is decisive over an ordered pair of states if their unanimous preference over the pair dictates social preference over the pair, and weakly decisive if this dictates either social preference or social indifference. An individual is decisive (or weakly decisive) when opposed if this holds when all other individuals have the opposite preference.

Definition A set $M \subset N$ is decisive (*or* weakly decisive) over (x, y) (written as $D_M(x, y)$) if $x\pi y$ (*or* $x\tilde{\pi} y$) whenever $x\pi^i y$ for each $i \in M$; it is decisive (*or* weakly decisive) when opposed over (x, y), that is $\bar{D}_M(x, y)$, if $x\pi y$ (*or* $x\tilde{\pi} y$) whenever $x\pi^i y$ for each $i \in M$ and $y\pi^i x$ for each $i \notin M$.

It is clear that the set of all individuals is decisive (and therefore weakly decisive) over all pairs of states because of unanimity. Similarly, no single individual can be decisive over all pairs because of impersonality (though he can be weakly decisive). If an individual is decisive over some pair (that is regardless of the preferences of others) then it is clear that he is decisive when opposed over that pair. In fact we might expect the reverse implication to hold as well, though this is less obvious. We now show this, and also the important extra property that an individual who is decisive when opposed over some pair is decisive over all pairs.

Proposition A.1 Under a social choice function which specifies a quasi-ordering an individual who is decisive (*or* weakly decisive) when opposed over some pair of states is decisive (*or* weakly decisive) over all pairs.

Proof Let $\bar{D}_{\{i\}}(x, y)$ (now written $\bar{D}_i(x, y)$) and assume $x\pi^i y \pi^i z$ with $y\pi^j x$ and $y\pi^j z$ for each $j \neq i$. Then $x\pi y$ by decisiveness and $y\pi z$ by unanimity, so that $x\pi z$ by quasi-transitivity; this holds whether $x\pi^j z$ or not, while the properties $y\pi^j x$ and $y\pi^j z$ are irrelevant by independence, so that $x\pi z$ whenever $x\pi^i z$, which is to say that $D_i(x, z)$. If instead we assume $z\pi^i x\pi^i y$ with $z\pi^j x$ and $y\pi^j x$ then in the same way we obtain $D_i(z, y)$, this and $D_i(x, z)$ being implied by the premise $\bar{D}_i(x, y)$. Then simply by changing the names of the states we also have $D_i(y, z)$ whenever $\bar{D}_i(x, z)$, and $D_i(y, x)$ whenever $\bar{D}_i(y, z)$. It follows from these four implications, and the fact that $\bar{D}_i(x, y)$ whenever $D_i(x, y)$, that $\bar{D}_i(x, y)$ implies $D_i(y, x)$. Then again changing names we have $\bar{D}_i(y, x)$ implies $D_i(x, y)$, so that $\bar{D}_i(y, x)$. All these results together show that i is decisive over all six pairs from $\{x, y, z\}$. Now consider an arbitrary set of states, and take $u, v \notin \{x, y, z\}$ from this (if $u \in \{x, y, z\}$ or $v \in \{x, y, z\}$ the result is obvious). Then considering $\{u, x, y\}$ we have $D_i\{x, u\}$ and thus $\bar{D}_i\{x, u\}$, which means that considering $\{u, v, x\}$ we have $D_i(u, v)$ and also $D_i(v, u)$. This proves the result for decisiveness; the argument for weak decisiveness is exactly parallel.

A.3 PARETO FUNCTION

We use this result to provide an axiomatic basis for the Pareto social choice function used in general equilibrium: specifically, we show that this is the only social choice function which specifies even a quasi-ordering. This is done by showing that some individual must be weakly decisive when opposed over some pair of states, and thus (from Proposition A.1) that this individual is weakly decisive over all pairs; then by impersonality all individuals must be weakly decisive over all pairs, from which it follows immediately that the social choice function is the Pareto function.

Proposition A.2 The Pareto social choice function is the only social choice function which specifies a quasi-ordering.

Proof Let $M \subset N$ be the smallest set which is decisive when opposed over some pair of states. Note that M exists, since N is decisive over all pairs by unanimity, but need not be unique; also M is not singleton, for otherwise all individuals would be decisive over all pairs, by Proposition A.1 and impersonality, which is impossible. Assume $\bar{D}_M(x, y)$ and $i \in M$, and, for some z, let $x\pi^i y \pi^i z$, $z\pi^j x \pi^j y$ for $i \neq j \in M$, and $y\pi^j z \pi^j x$ for $j \notin M$. Then $x\pi y$ because $\bar{D}_M(x, y)$, while $y\bar{\pi}z$ because otherwise $\bar{D}_{M-\{i\}}(z, y)$ and therefore M would not be smallest, so that $x\pi z$ by quasi-transitivity. This means that i is weakly decisive when opposed over (x, z), so that each individual is weakly decisive over all pairs, by Proposition A.1 and impersonality. It follows that $u\pi v$ only if $u\bar{\pi}^i v$ for each i, so that, by unanimity, $u\bar{\pi}v$ unless $v\bar{\pi}^i u$ for each i with strict preference for some, which is the Pareto function.

If the set of states is finite we can clearly arrange its elements along an axis so that, for some given individual, more preferred states are always to the right (or above) less preferred (and two indifferent states occupy the same place). Then in a society of two individuals the states socially preferred, socially 'worse', and socially indifferent (all according to this Pareto function) to some given state may be illustrated as in Figure A.1. This makes it clear that social preference in this sense only takes account of 'aggregate wellbeing', not its 'distribution'.

Since it is clear that the Pareto function is not fully transitive an immediate corollary to this proposition is the impossibility of obtaining any ordering from a social choice function.

Proposition A.3 There is no social choice function which specifies an ordering.

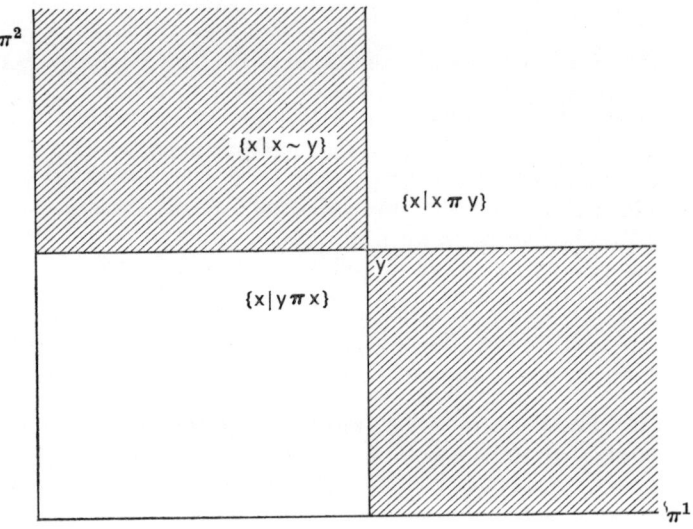

FIG. A.1

Proof If $x\pi^i y \pi^i z$ and $z\pi^j x \pi^j y$ the Pareto function gives $y \sim z$, $z \sim x$, and $x\pi y$, so is not transitive; the conclusion then follows immediately from Proposition A.2.

This impossibility theorem makes it clear why we can only require a quasi-ordering.

Notes
1 The framework of this appendix follows that of K. J. Arrow [*Social Choice and Individual Values*, New York, 1963], to whom the celebrated impossibility theorem is due. The Pareto function was originally proposed by V. Pareto [*Cours d'Économie Politique*, Lausanne, 1897], but the treatment here follows that of A. K. Sen [*Collective Choice and Social Welfare*, San Francisco, 1970].
2 The impossibility theorem may be strengthened by weakening some of the requirements for an aggregation function to be a social choice function. Specifically, unanimity may be weakened to require only that x be socially preferred to y when all individuals prefer x to y, while impersonality may be replaced by non-dictatorship, which only requires that there is no individual such that x is socially preferred to y whenever he prefers x to y. This is shown by Arrow and Sen.

Notation

Notation

a_i	slope of perceived demand curve for i	61
a	$(a_1, \ldots a_n)$	64
e	unit vector in E	8
E	n-dimensional extended Euclidean space	5
f_i	generating function for commodity i	64
f	$(f_1, \ldots f_n)$	64
h	typical consumer index	27
i	typical commodity index	13
I	identity mapping on E	11
k	typical producer index	38
l	number of producers	38
m	number of consumers	27
M	$\{1, \ldots m\}$	47
n	number of commodities	13
p_i	price of i	14
p	$(p_1, \ldots p_n)$	14
Q_m	m – simplex in E	8
r_i^h	h's resources of i	27
r^h	$(r_1^h, \ldots r_n^h)$	27
r_i	$\Sigma_h r_i^h$	28
r	$(r_1, \ldots r_n)$	28
R	$(r^1, \ldots r^h)$	28
s^{hk}	h's share in k	38
s^h	$(s^{h1}, \ldots s^{hl})$	39
S	$(s^1, \ldots s^m)$	39
u^h	utility function for $\bar{\pi}^h$ (also u)	16, 42
v^k	k's profit	38
v	$(v^1, \ldots v^l)$	39
x_i^h	h's consumption of i	14, 27
x^h	$(x_1^h, \ldots x_n^h)$	14, 27
x_i	$\Sigma_h x_i^h$	28
x	$(x_1, \ldots x_n)$	28
X	$(x^1, \ldots x^m)$	28
y_i^k	k's production of i	22, 38

y^k	$(y_1^k, \ldots y_n^k)$	22, 38
y_i	$\Sigma_k y_i^k$	39
y	$(y_1, \ldots y_n)$	39
Y	$(y^1, \ldots y^l)$	39
Y^k	k's production set	22, 38
z_i	excess demand for i	28
z	$(z_1, \ldots z_n)$	28
$\tilde{\pi}^h$	h's weak preference relation (also $\tilde{\pi}$)	14, 27
π^h	h's strict preference relation (also π)	14, 27
$\sim^h$	h's indifference relation (also $\sim$)	14, 27
Π	$(\tilde{\pi}^1, \ldots \tilde{\pi}^m)$	28
Γ	$(Y^1, \ldots Y^l)$	39
Ω	non-negative orthant in E	5
Ω_+	positive orthant in E	5

Index

Index

aggregate demand, 28
aggregate resources, 28
aggregate supply, 39
aggregation function, 99
— impersonality, 100
— independence, 100
— nondictatorship, 104
— unanimity, 99
Allingham, 69, 95, 96
allocation, 28
Arrow, 4, 11, 12, 26, 42, 81, 104
Aumann, 3, 41, 42, 54

biological feasibility, 26
Brouwer's theorem, 8
Brown, 54

characteristic root, 11
coalition, 47, 53
commodity, 13, 60
comparative statics, 3, 84
— of dynamic equilibrium, 95
— and Morishima property, 94
— and revealed preference, 84
— and stability, 91, 94
— and substitutability, 85, 86, 89
competitive equilibrium, 2, 28, 39
— and co-operative equilibrium, 48, 51, 53, 54
— and dynamic equilibrium, 68
— existence, 31, 40
— numeraire, 32, 40
— and optimum, 33, 34, 40
complements, 21
connectedness, 42
consumption, 14
convexity of equilibria, 38
— and revealed preference, 38, 40

co-operative equilibrium, 3, 47, 53
— asymptotic, 50, 54
— and competitive equilibrium, 48, 51, 53, 54
— and fairness, 50, 53
— and optimum, 47, 53
core, 47, 54
correspondence principle, 91

Debreu, 3, 11, 25, 26, 41, 54, 69
decisive, 100
— when opposed, 100
demand function (competitive), 17
— continuity, 19
— homogeneity, 19
— price effects, 20
derivative, 10
determinant, 11
distance, 6
dominant diagonality, 77
— and stability, 77
— and substitutability, 42
— and uniqueness, 42
dynamic equilibrium, 3, 58, 64
— comparative statics, 68
— and competitive equilibrium, 95
— existence, 65
— numeraire, 66
— and optimum, 67, 68
— stability, 80, 81

economy, 28, 39, 63
— and excess demand function, 41
— infinite, 41, 42
— replicated, 48, 53
Edgeworth, 3, 54
Edgeworth Box, 44
efficiency hypersurface, 24

excess demand function, 28
— continuity, 29, 39
— and economy, 41
— homogeneity, 29, 39
— unboundedness, 28, 40
— Walras' law, 29, 40
Euclidean space, 5
— extended, 5

fixed point, 8
Frobenius theorem, 11
function, 5
— continuous, 7
— differentiable, 10
— linear, 8
— quasi-concave/convex, 7

generating function, 58, 64

Hahn, 11, 12, 26, 42, 81, 96
Hicks, 3, 4, 95
Hicksian chain rule, 93
Hicksian Cross, 89
Hicksian laws, 86, 89
Hildenbrand, 12, 54
hyperplane, 8

indifference hypersurface, 16

Jacobian, 10

Kannai, 26
Klein, 12

le Chatelier principle, 86
limit, 6
Lyapounov function, 72

Malinvaud, 25
matrix, 10
— positive/negative, 11
— positive/negative definite, 11
— positive/negative diagonal, 11
— square, 11
— stable, 11
— symmetric, 11
maximum/minimum, 11
 inkowski theorem, 7

monopoly demand function, 62
— continuity, 63
Morishima, 3, 4, 95
Morishima property, 93
— and comparative statics, 94
— and stability, 93
Negishi, 81
Nikaido, 81
norm, 6
normal (to hyperplane), 8
normal commodity, 20, 87
numeraire, 32

optimum, 33, 40
— and competitive equilibrium, 33, 34, 40
— and co-operative equilibrium, 47, 53
— and dynamic equilibrium, 67, 68
ordering, 4, 15
— partial, 4
— and social choice function, 103

Pareto, 4, 104
Peleg, 41
perceived demand, 60
perceived revenue, 60
preference (individual), 14, 15
— Cobb-Douglas, 26
— continuity, 15
— convexity, 15
— homothetic, 68
— indifference, 14
— lexicographic, 26
— monotonicity, 15
— nonconvex, 41
— nonsatiation, 25
price, 14
production, 22
— efficient, 24
— personal, 52
production set, 22
— boundedness, 22
— continuity, 22
— convexity, 23
— free disposal, 23
— irreversibility, 26
— no free production, 23

profit, 24

quasi-ordering, 101
— and social choice function, 103
quasi-stability, 81
Quirk, 11

Rader, 12
real numbers, 5
— extended, 5
resources, 27
revealed preference, 38
— and convexity, 38, 40
— individual, 19
— and stability, 75
— and substitutability, 76, 81
Robinson, 54
Routh-Hurwitz theorem, 11

Samuelson, 3, 4, 95
Saposnik, 11
Scarf, 54
Sen, 4, 104
sequence, 6
set, 4
— bounded, 6
— closed, 6
— convex, 6
— weakly convex, 6
share, 38
similarity, 12
simplex, 8
social choice function, 100
— and ordering, 103
— Pareto, 100
— and quasi-ordering, 103
social preference, 4, 99
solution set, 54
stability, 3, 72
— and comparative statics, 91, 94
— and dominant diagonality, 77

— of dynamic equilibrium, 80, 81
— local, 73, 78
— and Morishima property, 93
— and no trade, 75
— nontatonnement, 81
— and revealed preference, 75
— and substitutability, 76
— unit-free, 79
Starr, 41
substitutability, 36, 88
— and comparative statics, 85, 86, 89
— and dominant diagonality, 42
— and revealed preference, 76, 81
— and stability, 76
— and uniqueness, 37, 40
— weak, 42
substitutes, 21
supply function, 24
— continuity, 25
— homogeneity, 24
— price effects, 25

tatonnement, 71
trace, 11

uniqueness, 36
— and dominant diagonality, 42
— and substitutability, 37, 40
utility function, 16
— existence, 16

Walras, 2, 3, 4, 41
Walras' law, 29
— weak, 64
wealth, 17, 28
Weierstrass' theorem, 7
Weintraub, 11, 12

Yaari, 41